# The Appropriations Law Answer Book

## A Q&A Guide to Fiscal Law

# The Appropriations Law Answer Book

## A Q&A Guide to Fiscal Law

**William G. Arnold**

MANAGEMENTCONCEPTS

MANAGEMENTCONCEPTSPRESS
8230 Leesburg Pike, Suite 800
Tysons Corner, VA 22182
(703) 790-9595
Fax: (703) 790-1371
www.managementconcepts.com



Printed in the United States of America

Library of Congress Control Number
2011943239
978-1-56726-362-6

10 9 8 7 6 5 4 3 2 1

# About the Author

**William G. Arnold** worked with the Department of Defense for 34 years, over 25 of which he spent in financial management. He has held positions as director of resource management, director of disbursing, and entitlements director with the Air Force and Defense Finance and Accounting Service. He is a certified defense financial manager with acquisition specialty (CDFM-A) from the American Society of Military Comptrollers, and in 1984 he was awarded the designation of certified cost analyst (CCA) by the Institute of Cost Analysis.

Mr. Arnold holds a Master of Arts degree in financial management from Central Michigan University. For many years he taught undergraduate classes in economics and finance at Park College.

Mr. Arnold is currently an instructor with Management Concepts. Course topics include an appropriations law seminar, appropriations law for business operations, the Antideficiency Act, budget execution, the Prompt Payment Act, voucher examination, performance budgeting, and enhanced defense financial management. Mr. Arnold is the author of *The Antideficiency Act Answer Book*, *The Prompt Payment Act Answer Book*, and *Performance Budgeting: What Works, What Doesn't*, all published by Management Concepts.

# Contents

# Preface

The manner in which agencies use government funds is under scrutiny as never before. The current fiscal crisis of large budget deficits, unfunded liabilities, and debt burden has made budget hawks out of even the most ardent advocates of large government spending. Widespread use of blogs and other social media has made de facto inspectors general out of uncounted citizens, who search for government misuse of taxpayer dollars.

The President has published executive orders on reducing the number of improper payments, and Congress passed the *Improper Payments Elimination and Reduction Act of 2010*. The pressure is on to use every federal dollar wisely and properly.

Yet federal personnel often don't know all the rules on the proper use of funds. What might seem like a logical, efficient action could very well be illegal. Thus, even personnel with the purest of intentions can run afoul of the myriad laws, rules, regulations, and decisions that govern the proper use of government funds.

I wrote this book to serve as a guide for anyone interested in using government funds properly and legally. That should include everyone who controls federal funds, and especially program managers, contracting personnel, funds certifiers, entitlement and certifying officials in paying offices, and auditors. Recipients of grants will also find it of interest. The book will help government purchase card holders and approvers, as well as all federal supervisors and managers, understand the situations in which they might be risking violation of one or more federal laws, rules, or policies. Auditors, too, should find the book a valuable resource when conducting both financial and performance audits.

This book is designed to be a basic "go-to" resource to answer fiscal law questions that arise in the federal workplace. It is based largely, though not solely, on the Government Accountability Office's *Principles of Federal Appropriations Law* (known as the Redbook). It is arranged in question-and-answer format, and it covers the questions that most often surface in agencies on a continuing basis. This book is an attempt to condense the 2,000+ pages of the Redbook into a short, pertinent, and usable resource that all government agencies will find valuable.

*The Appropriations Law Answer Book* is designed as a reference, enabling the reader to find the answer to a specific question. It is not designed to be read cover to cover. However, certain issues require several questions and answers to fully explore the topic. Care has been taken to group related questions in a logical flow. The reader is cautioned to read the entire section devoted to an issue to get a complete answer.

Although the questions and answers have been thoroughly researched and are as accurate and current as possible, do not rely on this book as a legal reference. Consult your agency's internal regulations and your legal counsel about specific issues.

I hope you find this book informative, helpful, thought-provoking, and, on occasion, entertaining.

*William G. Arnold*
February 2012

# Acknowledgments

Neither this book, nor any of the three previous books I've done in collaboration with Management Concepts, would have been possible without the expertise and support of Myra Strauss, Editorial Director at Management Concepts. She has been a delight to work with over the past several years, and I am deeply indebted to her.

The Management Concepts staff has also been wonderful during my nine-year association with the company. Margaret Linsday brought me into the company—what a great lady she is! I hesitate to mention the names of the rest of the staff who have been so helpful to me, for fear of leaving someone out. But certainly Hugh O'Hara, Andy Megas, Richard Lashford, Rick Hurley, Phil Davidson, Ken Boerum, Cathy Kreyche, Keith Hunter, and Janet McGowan deserve special praise for the support they have given me through the years.

Finally, to the many instructors I've taught with, and learned from—Tom Cablk, Doug Atkins, Ron Davidson, Joe Mullane, Rich Arns, Kent Miller, Milo Hall, John Reifsnyder, and Tom Stone—thank you for your counsel and friendship.

# Chapter 1
# Overview of Appropriations Law

This first chapter introduces basic appropriations law terminology and concepts. Readers unfamiliar with appropriations and their use would be well served to read this chapter in its entirety before addressing specific questions in later chapters. More seasoned personnel with a basic familiarity of the terms and concepts can get by without reading the entire chapter but might still find it useful should they encounter a specific issue that is addressed here.

## APPROPRIATIONS LAW BASICS

### 1. What is meant by the term *appropriations law*?

The term *federal appropriations law* or *federal fiscal law* means that body of law that governs the availability and use of federal funds.[1]

Federal funds are made available for obligation and expenditure by means of an appropriations act, or occasionally by other legislation, and the subsequent administrative actions that release appropriations to the spending agencies. The use or "availability" of appropriations once enacted and released—that is, the rules governing the purpose, amounts, manner, and timing of obligations and expenditures—is controlled by various authorities. These authorities include the terms of the appropriations act itself; any authorizing legislation; organic or enabling legislation, which prescribes a function or creates a program; general statutory provisions that allow or prohibit certain uses of appropriated funds; and general rules that have been developed over time through decisions of the comptroller general and the courts. These sources, together with provisions of the Constitution of the United States, form the basis of "appropriations law."[2]

## 2. Wouldn't it be simpler to just look for specific statutory prohibitions against the use of funds and operate on the premise that if an action isn't prohibited, it is authorized?

That approach would be far simpler, but it wouldn't be correct. A federal agency is a creature of law and can function only to the extent authorized by law. The Supreme Court has expressed what is perhaps the quintessential axiom of appropriations law as follows:

> The established rule is that the expenditure of public funds is proper only when authorized by Congress, not that public funds may be expended unless prohibited by Congress.[3]

That means that whenever a use of funds is proposed, the question should be: "What legal authority do I have to make this transaction?"

This is not to say that specific prohibitions do not exist. Congress specifically prohibits hundreds, if not thousands, of kinds of transactions in legislation it passes each year. Agencies must comply with such prohibitions. However, even absent a prohibition, agencies must have some legal authority to obligate and expend federal funds in a specific manner.

## 3. Who decides how federal funds are to be spent—the President or the Congress?

Congress has the "power of the purse." Congress appropriates funds and prescribes the conditions governing the use of those funds. This authority stems from the Constitution, most specifically from the so-called Appropriations Clause, the first part of article I, section 9, clause 7, which states:

> No money shall be drawn from the Treasury, but in Consequence of Appropriations made by Law . . . .[4]

The Appropriations Clause is the most important tool Congress has to rein in presidential power. Regardless of the nature of the payment—salaries, payments promised under a contract, payments ordered by a court, and so on—a federal agency may not make a payment from the United States Treasury unless Congress has made the funds available.

Thus, it is up to Congress to decide whether to provide funds for a particular program or activity, to put time limits on the use of such funds, and to fix the level of such funding.

The President and agencies do have administrative discretion on the use of funds appropriated by Congress, but such discretion is limited by the restrictions of the law. Thus, agencies are free to operate as they choose so long as they stay within the boundaries established by Congress.

## 4. How have the federal budget and appropriations processes evolved over time?

The first appropriations act, passed in 1789, illustrates how uncomplicated the process once was. The act contained only 141 words and just four appropriations for a total of $639,000. As the size and scope of the federal government grew, so did the complexity of the appropriations process.[5]

Until 1842 the calendar year and the government's fiscal year were identical. From 1842 until 1976, the fiscal year ran from July 1 to the following June 30. Since fiscal year 1977, it has run from October 1 to September 30.[6]

Appropriations committees first appeared in the House and Senate during the Civil War. These committees took over appropriations duties from the House Ways and Means Committee and Senate Finance Committee.[7]

Following World War I, Congress passed the *Budget and Accounting Act of 1921*.[8] Prior to 1921 agencies had made individual requests for appropriations. The Act required the President to submit a national budget each year and restricted the authority of agencies to present their own proposals. It also established the Bureau of the Budget (now called the Office of Management and Budget, or OMB) and provided Congress additional oversight capability over fiscal matters by creating the General Accounting Office (now called the Government Accountability Office, or GAO).[9]

As the federal budget became more complex, it became apparent that Congress was deeply involved in the appropriations process but had little involvement in the budget process. In response to this realization, Congress passed the *Congressional Budget Act of 1974*. One of the fundamental objectives of the Act was to establish a process through which Congress could systematically consider the total federal budget and determine priorities for allocating budget resources. The Act set up a detailed calendar for the phases of the congressional budget and appropriations processes. It created the House and Senate Budget Committees and the Congressional Budget Office. It was also the law that changed the fiscal year to its current October through September time frame.[10]

## 5. What are the steps involved in budget and appropriations processes?

GAO describes five phases in the "life cycle" of an appropriation:[11]

- Executive budget formulation and transmittal
- Congressional action
- Budget execution and control
- Audit and review
- Account closing.

An overview of the five phases follows.

**Executive budget formulation and transmittal.** This is a long process, often beginning years before a budget is ready to be submitted to Congress. Agencies, with oversight by OMB, develop estimates to satisfy operational requirements for a given fiscal year. OMB consolidates all the executive branch budgets, along with budgets submitted by the legislative and judicial branches, into the "Budget of the United States Government."[12] This is normally called the President's Budget, and it must be submitted to Congress by the first Monday in February of each year, for the following fiscal year.[13]

**Congressional action.** After receiving the President's Budget, the Congressional Budget Office submits to the House and Senate Budget Committees a report containing its analysis of fiscal policy and budget priorities. The Budget Committees then hold hearings and prepare their versions of a concurrent resolution, which is the overall budget plan against which individual appropriation bills are to be evaluated. Congress then passes a concurrent budget resolution that includes a breakdown for each major budget function.[14]

Meanwhile, the House Appropriations Committee (and its 12 subcommittees) has been studying the appropriation requests and evaluating the performance of the agencies under its purview. Each subcommittee conducts hearings at which federal officials give testimony concerning the costs and achievements of the various programs administered by their agencies and provide detailed justifications for their funding requests. Eventually, each subcommittee reports a single appropriation bill for consideration by the entire committee and then the full House membership.[15]

After individual appropriation bills are passed by the House, they are sent to the Senate. A similar process takes place in the Senate, culminating with passage by the full Senate.

If the House and Senate version are different, which is almost always the case, a conference committee composed of representatives from the House and Senate Appropriations Committees is formed with the purpose of resolving all differences. The conference committee produces a conference report, which must then be passed by the full House and Senate.[16]

Following passage by Congress, the bill, called an "enrolled" bill, is presented to the President for signature. Upon his signature the bill becomes an appropriations act and the appropriations contained therein become "available."[17]

The *Congressional Budget Act* envisioned this congressional process to be completed by October 1, the beginning of the fiscal year.[18]

**Budget execution and control.** During this phase an agency's task is to spend the money Congress has given it to carry out the objectives of its program legislation. OMB apportions, or distributes, budgeted amounts to the executive branch agencies, thereby making funds in appropriations accounts (held at the Treasury Department) available for obligation. Budget authority is normally apportioned by time periods (quarterly is most common) and is intended to achieve an effective and orderly use of available budget authority and to reduce the need for supplemental or deficiency appropriations.[19]

Each agency then makes allotments of its apportioned authority. An allotment is a delegation of authority to agency officials that allows them to incur obligations.[20]

Agency officials then obligate the funds allotted to them to carry out their assigned duties. An obligation is a legally binding agreement between the government and another party that promises payment to the other party in exchange for the provision of needed goods or services.[21]

Ultimately, payment is made to liquidate obligations. Such payments made to entities external to the federal government are called outlays.[22]

**Audit and review.** There are a number of audit and review requirements:

- Every federal agency has a responsibility to ensure that its use of public funds complies with appropriations acts and other laws. An internal audit program helps agencies comply with this requirement.
- Ensuring the legality of proposed payments is also a basic responsibility of agency certifying officers.
- The *Chief Financial Officers Act of 1990* provides for the preparation and audit of financial statements by the largest agencies.
- Treasury is required to submit an annual financial statement for the executive branch that has been audited by GAO.
- GAO also regularly audits federal programs.[23]

**Account closing.** At midnight on the last day of an appropriation's period of availability, the appropriation account expires and is no longer available for incurring new obligations. However, unexpended balances, both obligated and unobligated, retain limited availability for an additional five years. This expired availability is for the purpose of paying obligations incurred prior to the account's expiration and adjusting obligations that were previously unrecorded or underrecorded. After five years, the expired account is closed and the balances remaining are canceled.[24]

## 6. You mentioned 12 subcommittees each producing an appropriations bill. Does that mean there are only 12 appropriations?

There are 12 appropriations acts each year, but each act contains multiple appropriations. Thus, hundreds of appropriations are contained within the 12 appropriations acts.

The 12 appropriations acts are as follows:[25]

- Agriculture
- Commerce/Justice/Science
- Defense
- Energy and Water
- Financial Services
- Homeland Security
- Interior and Environment
- Labor/Health and Human Services/Education
- Legislative Branch
- Military Construction/Veterans Affairs
- State/Foreign Operations
- Transportation/Housing and Urban Development.

Smaller agencies not listed show up in various acts as "Independent and Related Agencies."

## 7. Where does GAO fit into the appropriations process?

GAO, part of the legislative branch, was created by the *Budget and Accounting Act of 1921*. That act abolished the offices of the Comptroller of the Treasury and six Auditors and transferred their functions to the comptroller general, who heads GAO. Among these functions was issuing legal decisions to agency officials concerning the availability and use of appropriated funds.[26]

## 8. Are comptroller general decisions binding on the executive branch?

It depends on whom you ask.

GAO certainly thinks they are binding. Quoting from GAO's *Principles of Federal Appropriations Law*: "A decision regarding an account of the government is binding on the executive branch and on the Comptroller General himself, but is not binding on a private party who, if dissatisfied, retains whatever recourse to the courts he would otherwise have had." Congress clearly intended its decisions to be binding. 31 U.S.C. 3526(d) states that "on settling an account of the Government, the balance certified by the Comptroller General is conclusive on the executive branch of the Government."[27]

The Justice Department Office of Legal Counsel (OLC) disagrees. That office has a "longstanding precedent that GAO's decisions are not binding on the Executive Branch." In a 2009 memorandum the Deputy Assistant Attorney General referenced several previous memoranda and OLC decisions on the subject. Among the quotations are the following:[28]

> The Comptroller General is an officer of the Legislative Branch. Because GAO is part of the Legislative Branch, Executive Branch agencies are not bound by GAO's legal advice.
>
> Our Office has on many occasions issued opinions and memoranda concluding that GAO decisions are not binding on the Executive Branch agencies and that the opinions of the Attorney General and this Office are controlling.
>
> Although the opinions and legal interpretations of the GAO and the Comptroller General often provide helpful guidance on appropriations matters and related issues, they are not binding upon departments, agencies, or officers of the executive branch.
>
> This Office has never regarded the legal opinions of the Comptroller General as binding upon the Executive.

The Office of Legal Counsel considers GAO's assertion that its decisions are binding on the executive branch to be an infringement on the constitutional separation of the executive and legislative branches.

## 9. What is an agency head or certifying officer to do if GAO and OLC disagree? Whose opinion counts?

Happily, GAO and OLC are in agreement most of the time. In fact, OLC often seeks or references GAO's opinions. However, when OLC specifically disagrees with GAO and issues its own decision, agency heads need to remember whom they work for—the executive branch. Certifying officers are in a more precarious position. GAO grants or denies relief of liability for all certifying officers, except for the armed forces. Therefore, the safest course of action for such non-armed forces certifying officers is to follow GAO guidance while trying to avoid trouble in their own agency.

## 10. If an agency ignores GAO decisions, what happens?

The comptroller general has no power to enforce decisions but does have the ear of Congress. Agency officials who act contrary to comptroller general decisions might have to respond to congressional appropriations and program oversight committees.[29] Congress might also pass clarifying legislation reiterating GAO's position, perhaps including some onerous reporting requirements. Remember that agencies disregard GAO, appropriations committees, and oversight committees at their own peril. The power of the purse is a mighty weapon that Congress is not reluctant to use.

## 11. How are comptroller general decisions annotated?

Two basic styles of annotation are used. Older decisions that were published in the *Decisions of the Comptroller General* volumes are cited by volume, page number on which the decision begins, and year; for example, 31 Comp. Gen. 350 (1952).[30] This means you go to volume 31 of the *Decisions* and open to page 350. Unpublished decisions before 1994 and all decisions thereafter are cited by file number and date. They take the form B-123456, date. Whenever you see a "B" followed by a six-digit number and a date, you know you are looking at a reference to a comptroller general decision.

## 12. How would someone research a comptroller general decision?

Normally the first place to look is in the relevant chapter of the Redbook, GAO's *Principles of Federal Appropriations Law*. Failing that, GAO's website, www.gao.gov, has a search engine for comptroller general decisions. If you have the reference number, for example, "B-312477, April 15, 2007," type it into the search engine and the decision will be displayed. If you don't have the reference number, use the search engine by entering some key words about the topic at hand, and decisions containing those words will be displayed.

## 13. What other forms of annotation is someone likely to encounter?

In addition to comptroller general decisions, the most common references will be to public laws, the *United States Code*, and the *Code of Federal Regulations*.

Public laws are the actual acts passed by Congress. Their annotation takes the form P.L. 109–155. In this example, the 109 represents the number of the Congress that passed the law, and the 155 means this was the 155$^{th}$ law passed by the 109$^{th}$ Congress. Each Congress lasts two years, beginning with the first Congress back in 1789–1790. The current Congress is the 112$^{th}$ Congress (2011–2012).

The *United States Code* contains an updated compilation of all permanent provisions of public laws previously passed; thus, it is our body of permanent federal law. In congressional parlance, "permanent" means that the provision stays in effect forever, or until some future Congress changes it. Permanent provisions typically contain some words of futurity to indicate that Congress intends them to be permanent; such words include *hereafter*, *thereafter*, *henceforth*, and *after the effective date of this act*. The *United States Code* is broken up into 51 titles, or chapters, each dealing with a different aspect of the government.[31] For example, Title 5 is about administration and personnel, Title 10 contains laws about the armed forces, and Title 31 is about money and banking. Annotation takes the form of 31 U.S.C. 1341. That means it is section 1341 of Title 31. The section number is merely a placeholder that allows one to find it within the specified title.

The *Code of Federal Regulations* has a similar form of annotation. For example, 5 CFR 1315 refers to Part 1315 of Title 5 of the *Code*. Regulations are written by agencies[32] and published as prescribed in the *Administrative Procedures Act*. There is not a one-to-one correlation between *United States Code* and *Code of Federal Regulations* title numbers, so one needs a separate list to determine the content of each of the titles.

## APPROPRIATIONS TERMINOLOGY

### *Budget Authority*

#### 14. The terms *budget authority* and *obligation authority* are often used as synonyms. Are they the same thing?

There is a difference between the two, but most of the time there won't be any confusion if the terms are used interchangeably.

Congress finances federal programs and activities by providing budget authority. *Budget authority* is a general term referring to various forms of authority provided by law to enter into financial obligations that will result in immediate or future outlays of government funds. Budget authority flows from Congress to an agency. Obligation authority, on the other hand, is created when an agency provides an individual the authority to enter into obligations that will result in outlays. Most of the time the dividing line between budget authority and obligation authority is the issuance of an allotment. So an agency receives budget authority from OMB in the form of an apportionment, and the agency then uses an allotment to pass on obligation authority to the responsible funds holder.

#### 15. Is there more than one form of budget authority?

GAO describes six categories of budget authority:[33]

- *Appropriations*—Appropriations are the most common form of budget authority. An *appropriation* is defined as the authority given to federal agencies to incur obligations and to make payments from Treasury for specified purposes.

While other forms of budget authority may authorize the incurring of obligations, the authority to incur obligations by itself is not sufficient to authorize payments from the Treasury. The previously mentioned "Appropriations Clause" in the Constitution requires an appropriation to support all payments. Thus, when obligations are ultimately paid, they must be paid from an appropriation.

- *Contract authority*—Contract authority is a form of budget authority that permits obligations to be incurred in advance of appropriations. It is not to be confused with the inherent authority that each agency possesses to enter into contracts; rather, it is an authority that depends on the availability of funds.

  Contract authority itself is not an appropriation. It provides the authority to enter into binding contracts but not the funds to make payments under those contracts. Therefore, obligations made under contract authority must be liquidated, or paid, from a subsequent appropriation.

- *Borrowing authority*—This type of budget authority permits agencies to incur obligations and make payments to liquidate the obligations out of borrowed moneys. The authority may allow borrowing from the Treasury, the public, the Federal Financing Bank, or some combination of these sources. Borrowing from the Treasury is the most common form and is also known as public debt financing.

- *Monetary credits*—This is a seldom used form of budget authority that allows the government to use monetary credits, rather than money, to acquire property such as land or mineral rights. The seller is given credits that represent the selling price, which may then be used pay the government amounts owed—for example, income taxes.

- *Loan and loan guarantee authority*—Agencies use this form of budget authority when they have been granted the authority to incur direct loan obligations or to incur loan guarantee commitments. The concept of direct loans is familiar to everyone; a loan guarantee, on the other hand, needs further explanation.

  A loan guarantee is any guarantee, insurance, or other pledge with respect to the payment of all or a part of the principal or interest on any debt obligation of a nonfederal borrower to a nonfederal lender. The government does not know whether or to what extent it may be required to honor its guarantee until the borrower defaults. Therefore, loan guarantees are contingent liabilities that may not be recorded as obligations until the contingency occurs. During the interim, the amount of the loan guarantee is carried in the accounting records as a commitment.

- *Offsetting receipts*—The name of this form of budget authority is somewhat misleading and does not do justice to the scope of its existence. The federal government receives money from many sources in a variety of contexts. Moneys received are called collections, and they are broken into two major categories—governmental receipts and offsetting collections.
  - Governmental receipts (also called budget receipts) are collections resulting from the government's exercising its sovereign or regulatory powers. Examples are tax receipts, customs duties, and court fines.
  - Offsetting collections are the funds resulting from business-type or market-oriented activities, such as the sale of goods or services to the public, and from intragovernmental transactions. Offsetting collections are divided into two categories.
    - First is offsetting collections credited to appropriation or fund accounts. These are collections that may be deposited in an appropriation or fund account under the control of the agency and are then available for obligation by the agency, subject to the purpose and time limitations of the receiving account.
    - Second is offsetting receipts, which are offsetting collections that are deposited into a receipt account. These funds are not available to the agency that collected them.

## *Types of Appropriations*

### 16. I've heard appropriations described in many ways. Annual, no-year, current, indefinite, and expired are just a few. What do all of these terms mean?

There are many ways to look at appropriations (or other forms of budget authority for that matter), and the result is a large number of terms that can be quite daunting. Let's break it down into four classifications, each with subordinate elements:

1. Duration:[34]
   a. One-year appropriation: An appropriation that is available for obligation only during a specific fiscal year. This is the most common type of appropriation. It is also known as a fiscal year or annual appropriation.
   b. Multiple-year appropriation: An appropriation that is available for obligation for a definite period of time in excess of one fiscal year.

      Note: One-year and multiple-year appropriations are collectively known as fixed-term appropriations.
   c. No-year appropriation: An appropriation that is available for obligation for an indefinite period. A no-year appropriation is usually identified by appropriation language such as "to remain available until expended."
2. Presence or absence of monetary limits:[35]
   a. Definite appropriation: An appropriation of a specific amount of money.
   b. Indefinite appropriation: An appropriation of an unspecified amount of money. It might appropriate future receipts, the amount of which is unknown until some future date. In other cases, it might appropriate "such sums as may be necessary" for a given purpose.
3. Permanency:[36]
   a. Current appropriation: An appropriation made by Congress in, or immediately prior to, the fiscal year or years during which it is available for obligation.
   b. Permanent appropriation: A "standing" appropriation which, once made, is always available for specified purposes and does not require repeated action by Congress to authorize its use. For example, legislation authorizing an agency to retain and use offsetting receipts is a common form of a permanent appropriation.

4. Availability for new obligations:[37]
   a. Unexpired appropriation (also referred to as a current appropriation or an available appropriation): An appropriation that is available for incurring new obligations.
   b. Expired appropriation: An appropriation that is no longer available to incur new obligations. It is still available for liquidations of and adjustments to obligations properly incurred before the period of availability expired.
   c. Canceled appropriation: An appropriation whose account is closed. In this phase the appropriation is no longer available for obligation or expenditure for any purpose.

## 17. What about operations that don't receive direct appropriations from Congress—for example, working capital funds? Are they considered appropriations?

Indeed they are. Every revolving fund and special deposit fund was established pursuant to a statute. Those implementing statutes that made amounts in those funds available for obligation and expenditure are permanent appropriations.[38] Money may be withdrawn from the Treasury only if Congress appropriates it—that's a constitutional restriction. Therefore, the authority for an agency to obligate or expend collections without further congressional action amounts to a continuing appropriation or permanent appropriation of the collections. If these sorts of funds were not considered appropriations, they wouldn't be able to operate because they would never be able to spend any of the money collected.

## 18. My agency receives several appropriations each year. Some are very general—for example, operating expenses. Others are much more specific—laptop computers and software, for instance. What are the rules when you have what seem to be overlapping purposes of the appropriations?

An appropriation made for a specific purpose is available for that purpose to the exclusion of a more general appropriation, which might otherwise be used for that purpose.[39] Using the example given, absent your specific appropriation for laptops and software, you would rightfully use your operating expenses appropriations to buy computers and software. But, because you have a more specific appropriation available, you may not use your operating expenses appropriation to buy laptops or software. You must use the specific appropriation. This continues to be true even if you exhaust the specific appropriation. Lack of sufficient funding in a specific appropriation does not confer the right to revert to a general appropriation as a backup.

## 19. In the previous example, if I run out of money in my laptop appropriation, couldn't I just move some money from my operating expenses appropriation?

Not without statutory authority. What you just described is a transfer—moving funds from one appropriation to another. The word *transfer* is quite often preceded by the word *illegal*. The prohibition against transfer is in 31 U.S.C. 1532, which starts: "An amount available under law may be withdrawn from one appropriation account and credited to another or to a working fund only when authorized by law."[40] That Congress would prohibit transfers seems obvious. If agencies were allowed to transfer funds between appropriations at will, there would be no point in Congress's breaking funds out into appropriations as it does. Congress often does provide agencies limited transfer authority. This is normally spelled out in the general provisions section of the agency annual appropriations act. Unauthorized transfers result in purpose law violations and augmentation of the receiving appropriation. Ultimately, they can mean violations of the *Antideficiency Act*. All of these negative outcomes are discussed in detail in later chapters.

## 20. If I can't move money between appropriations, may I at least move funds between various uses within an appropriation?

Yes, you may. This is called reprogramming. Reprogramming is the use of funds in an appropriation account for purposes other than those contemplated at the time of appropriation. In other words, it is the shifting of funds from one purpose or object to another within an appropriation. The authority to reprogram is implicit in an agency's responsibility to manage its funds;[41] no statutory authority is needed. However, appropriations acts often place limits or thresholds on the amount an agency may reprogram and tie reprogramming actions to reports to oversight committees. Obviously, agencies must comply with all such statutory requirements and prohibitions.

### 21. Suppose I have two appropriations that are equally general (or equally specific). I can make a case that either appropriation is the logical source of funding for a particular item. Which do I use, or do I just use whichever one is more convenient or has more money in it?

This situation is rare, but it does occur from time to time. The rule is that when two appropriations are available for the same purpose and neither is more specific to that purpose, the agency selects which one to charge for the item in question. However, once that selection is made, the agency must continue to use the same appropriation for that purpose.[42] This is sometimes referred to as the "pick and stick" rule: Pick an appropriation and stick with it. An agency may change its pick only by notifying Congress of its intention to switch at the beginning of the fiscal year.

## APPROPRIATIONS VERSUS AUTHORIZATIONS

### 22. My agency receives an annual authorization act, which includes statements that "authorize the appropriation" of a certain dollar amount for a particular program or purpose. Do these laws give my agency budget authority?

As a general proposition, the answer is "no." With very rare exceptions, authorization acts do not provide any money.[43]

There are actually two kinds of legislation that must be distinguished from appropriations acts. The first is organic or enabling legislation, which creates an agency, establishes a program, or prescribes a function. This legislation provides the legal basis for conducting a program or activity, but it does not provide budget authority to do so. The second is appropriation authorization legislation, which authorizes the appropriation of funds to implement the organic legislation. Often the authorization language is part of the organic legislation, or it may be separate.[44]

There is no general requirement that an appropriations act be preceded by a specific authorization act. There are a limited number of statutory requirements for authorizations in specific situations. However, the rules of the House of Representatives prohibit appropriations for expenditure not previously authorized by law. The effect of such rules subjects an offending appropriation to a point of order but does not prohibit passage and implementation if no point of order is raised.

An authorization act's "authority to appropriate" language is basically a directive to Congress itself, which Congress is free to follow or alter (up or down) in the subsequent appropriations act.[45]

## 23. Authorization and appropriations acts are sometimes in conflict. Which one do we follow when that happens?

Most of the time the authorizing committees and the appropriations committees work closely to avoid conflicts, but it is not unusual for differences to occur. The first thing an agency does is try to harmonize—to give maximum effect to both acts whenever possible.[46] If that is not possible, a good rule to follow is this: If the difference between an authorization and appropriations act involves purpose, time, or amount, the appropriations act trumps the authorization act.[47] For example, suppose an authorization act authorized the appropriation of $50,000 to be available for obligation for three years to buy three trucks. The corresponding appropriations act appropriates $35,000 to be available for two years to buy two trucks. The appropriation has changed the scope of the buy—the purpose, the time limit for availability, and the amount. The agency is limited to spending $35,000, can buy only two trucks, and has two years to obligate the funds.

## 24. What if the conflict doesn't have to do with purpose, time, or amount and is otherwise irreconcilable?

Another example will illustrate: An authorization act authorizes the appropriation of $5 million, to be available for obligation for five years, to build a new headquarters building in Silver Spring, Maryland, and it is to be made of brick. The appropriations act appropriates $5 million, to be available for five years, to build a new headquarters building in Arlington, Virginia, and it is to be blue in color.

In this case, the purpose (headquarters building), time (five years), and amount ($5 million) are not in conflict. However, two aspects of the building—building materials/color and location—are in apparent conflict. The agency can give effect to both laws by building the new headquarters out of blue bricks, thus harmonizing those differences in the language. The location, on the other hand, is irreconcilable; it can't be in both Maryland and Virginia. In this case, the more recent statute, as the latest expression of Congress, governs. Whichever statute became law last prevails. The logic is simple: The same 535 Members of Congress that passed the first law also passed the second law. What can we conclude if the first law said Maryland and the second law said Virginia? Congress must have changed its mind. Remember that this "last in line" principle is applied only when two statutes cannot be reconciled in any reasonable manner, and then only to the extent of the conflict.[48]

# INTERPRETING LEGISLATION

## 25. Often when a question arises, reading the organic, authorization, or appropriations act doesn't answer the question. The law might be incomplete or unclear. How does one go about interpreting laws to determine whether an action is authorized and lawful?

A voluminous amount of literature is devoted to the area of statutory construction. The goal of statutory construction is to determine and give effect to the intent of the legislation. Although the goal is simple, achieving it is complex and often controversial.[49]

The primary vehicle for determining legislative intent is the language of the statute itself.[50] Secondarily, legislative history is often consulted. Chances are good that Congress never contemplated the particular issues an agency is confronted with and formed no intent about them. Congress sometimes deliberately leaves issues ambiguous because it lacks a sufficient consensus to resolve them in the law.

At the risk of oversimplifying a very complex subject, I will address a few basic canons of statutory construction.

**Plain meaning rule.**[51] You start with the language of the statute. If the meaning is clear from the language, there is no need to resort to legislative history or other extraneous sources. In other words, we apply the common meaning of words and normal rules of sentence construction and grammar to arrive at a meaning. We don't apply some "creative" meaning to words or construction because it better suits our purposes.

Examples abound:

- An appropriation for topographical surveys in the United States was not available for topographical surveys in Puerto Rico. By definition, "the United States" does not include Puerto Rico. If Congress had intended to include Puerto Rico and other locations, it would have specified "in the United States, territories, and commonwealths."
- An appropriation to install an electrical generating plant in the custom house building in Baltimore could not be used to install the plant in a nearby post office building, even though the plant would serve both buildings and thereby reduce operating expenses. Thus, saving money is not an excuse to violate statutory language.
- An appropriation for the "replacement" of state roads could not be used to make "improvements" on them.
- Funds provided for the "modification" of existing dams for safety purposes could not be used to construct a new dam, even as part of an overall safety strategy.

Consulting a dictionary is the commonsense starting point for determining the plain meaning of a word.[52] Further, when Congress uses the same term in more than one place in the statute, apply the same meaning to that word in each instance unless there is clear evidence Congress intended a different meaning.[53] In other words, don't apply different definitions to the same word in different contexts because doing so better suits your desire.

**Errors in statutes.** Sometimes what is clearly a technical or typographical error occurs in a statute. If the intent is obvious, such errors are usually ignored or repaired. For example, an appropriation provided funds for payments in conjunction with an election held on "November fifth, 1890." The election actually was held on November 4. Recognizing the "evident intention of Congress," the comptroller general's decision held that the appropriation was available for the payments associated with the November 4 election.[54]

If the error is in an amount appropriated, however, the rule above generally does not apply. A 1979 appropriations act included $36 million for a specific purpose. Both the House and Senate bills and various committee reports specified only $35 million. The comptroller general held that despite being an apparent typographical error, the number is the number, and $36 million had been appropriated.[55]

**Avoiding absurd consequences.** The generally accepted principle is that the literal language of a statute will not be followed if it would produce a result inconsistent with clearly expressed congressional intent, that is, an "absurd consequence."[56]

A statute making it a criminal offense to obstruct or retard a mail carrier does not apply to a sheriff arresting a mail carrier who has been indicted for murder.[57] It would be an "absurd consequence" to require the sheriff to wait until the carrier had completed his rounds before making the arrest. Likewise, a statute making it a felony to break out of jail does not apply to a prisoner who broke out because the jail was on fire.

The absurd consequence test should be used sparingly and is not always easy to apply. What strikes one person as absurd might be good law to another.[58]

## 26. You previously mentioned "legislative history" as a source for interpreting statutory language. How does that work?

Legislative history is the body of congressionally generated written documents relating to a bill from the time of introduction to the time of enactment. There are two ways to use these documents. One is to examine them, searching for the meaning and intent of the legislation. The other is to examine the evolution of the bill's language through the legislative process. Changes made to a bill during its consideration are often instructive in determining its final meaning.

## 27. Where do you start when examining legislative history?

There is a hierarchy, or "order of persuasiveness," to use as a guideline.

- *Conference committee reports*—The most authoritative single source of legislative history is the conference report.[59] The reason the conference report occupies the highest rung on the ladder is that it must be voted on and adopted by both houses of Congress and thus is the only legislative history document that can be said to reflect the will of both houses.
- *Committee reports*—Next in line are the reports of the legislative committees that considered the bill and reported it out to their respective houses.[60] For appropriations bills, these would be the Appropriations Committee reports.
- *Floor debates*—Proceeding downward on the ladder, after committee reports come floor debates.[61] However, statements made in the course of floor debates are regarded as suspect because they reflect the views and motives of the individual members making them.
- *Hearings*—Hearings occupy the bottom rung of the legislative history ladder.[62] They can be valuable in defining the problem Congress is addressing and presenting opposing points of view. As legislative history, they are the least persuasive form. They reflect the personal opinions of the witnesses. It is generally impossible to attribute those opinions to anyone in Congress, let alone Congress

as a whole. If it can be shown that the language of a bill was revised in direct response to the testimony, its value as legislative history increases.

- *Post-enactment statements*—Not even on the ladder of legislative history are post-enactment statements. The Supreme Court, other courts, and GAO follow the principle that post-enactment statements do not constitute legislative history.[63] For example, they will not be persuaded by statements by a bill's sponsor made on a talk show after the law has been passed.

## NOTES

1. U.S. Government Accountability Office, *Principles of Federal Appropriations Law, Volume I* (GAO-04-261SP), Chap.1, 1-2.
2. Ibid.
3. Ibid.
4. Ibid., 1-3.
5. Ibid., 1-14.
6. Ibid., 1-15.
7. Ibid.
8. Ibid.
9. Ibid., 1-16.
10. Ibid., 1-17.
11. Ibid., 1-24.
12. Ibid., 1-25.
13. Ibid., 1-27.
14. Ibid., 1-28.
15. Ibid.
16. Ibid., 1-29.
17. Ibid.
18. Ibid.
19. Ibid., 1-31.
20. Ibid.
21. U.S. Government Accountability Office, *A Glossary of Terms Used in the Federal Budget Process* (GAO-05-734SP), September 2005.

22. Ibid.
23. U.S. Government Accountability Office, *Principles,* Chap. 1, 1-35.
24. Ibid., 1-37.
25. http://thomas.loc.gov/home/approp/app12.html
26. U.S. Government Accountability Office, *Principles,* Chap. 1, 1-39.
27. Ibid., 1-40.
28. http://www.justice.gov/olc/2009/sba-hubzone-opinion082109.pdf
29. U.S. Government Accountability Office, *Principles,* Chap. 1, 1-40.
30. Ibid., 1-45.
31. http://uscode.house.gov/about/info.shtml
32. Ibid.
33. U.S. Government Accountability Office, *Principles,* Chap. 2, 2-4.
34. Ibid., 2-13.
35. Ibid., 2-14.
36. Ibid.
37. Ibid., 2-15.
38. Ibid., 2-17.
39. Ibid., 2-21.
40. Ibid., 2-25.
41. Ibid., 2-30.
42. Ibid., 2-23.
43. Ibid., 2-40.
44. Ibid.
45. Ibid., 2-41.
46. Ibid., 2-44.
47. Ibid., 2-46 – 2-56.
48. Ibid., 2-57.
49. Ibid., 2-72.
50. Ibid.
51. Ibid., 2-74.
52. Ibid., 2-89.
53. Ibid.
54. Ibid., 2-79.
55. Ibid., 2-80.

56. Ibid.
57. Ibid., 2-81.
58. Ibid.
59. Ibid., 2-98.
60. Ibid., 2-99.
61. Ibid., 2-100.
62. Ibid., 2-102.
63. Ibid., 2-104.

# Chapter 2
## Purpose

This chapter introduces the concept of the "availability" of appropriations. Comptroller general decisions are often stated in terms of whether appropriated funds are or are not "legally available" for a given obligation or expenditure. This is just another way of saying that a given item is or is not a legal expenditure. Legal availability depends on three factors:[1]

1. The purpose of the obligation or expenditure must be authorized.
2. The obligation must occur within the time limits applicable to the appropriation.
3. The obligation and expenditure must be within the amounts Congress has established.

Thus, three elements—purpose, time, and amount—control availability. All three must be met for the transaction to be legal. This chapter discusses availability in terms of purpose; Chapters 3 and 4 cover time and amount.

### 28. Is there a specific statute that prescribes the "purpose" element of availability?

The most fundamental statute dealing with purpose is the so-called "purpose law," found at 31 U.S.C. 1301(a):

> Appropriations shall be applied only to the objects for which the appropriations were made except as otherwise provided by law.[2]

This law is simple and concise, yet it is the source of more Comptroller General decisions than the time and amount elements combined. Very simply, it says that public funds may be used only for the purposes for which they were appropriated. It prohibits charging authorized items to the wrong appropriation, and it also prohibits charging unauthorized items to any appropriation.[3]

## 29. What is meant in the purpose law by the term *object*?

Objects include programs, projects, and activities carried out by agencies. Included are all physical goods, services, and even intangible items like patents, mineral rights, and the like. An object is anything the government wants to acquire—the resources an agency needs to carry out its functions.

## 30. How much latitude does an agency have in interpreting the purpose of an appropriation?

The more general the language of the appropriation, the more latitude, or discretion, the agency may employ. However, as discussed in the previous chapter, agencies are bound by the language in the appropriations act and may not use creative and far-fetched interpretations if the statutory language is clear. For example, funds appropriated for "modification of existing dams" may not be used to build new dams, even if doing so improves safety.[4] If an agency wants to build a new dam, it needs Congress to appropriate some "new dam money."

## 31. Suppose there would be a big cost savings to the government if an agency slightly sidesteps the language of the appropriation. Is that justification to do something different?

Saving money is not an excuse to break the law. If the proposed use of funds is inconsistent with statutory language, it is improper, regardless of any savings that might accrue.[5] For example, the Federal Aviation Administration (FAA) had an appropriation to construct its own roads for access to FAA facilities. Because of the restrictive language in the appropriation, the FAA could not use the funds to improve existing county-owned roads, even though the improved roads would have provided the necessary access and would have been much less expensive.

In such instances, agencies may request that Congress modify the appropriation language to garner the savings. Failing that, the appropriation language must be followed.

## 32. I work in a working capital fund and have often heard that we can use our money for most any purpose. In other words, because working capital fund balances were not directly appropriated by Congress, they are just cash, to be used at the discretion of the agency. Is that true?

That is not true. Although working capital funds do not normally receive direct appropriations from Congress, they are still appropriated funds. Remember the discussion in the previous chapter: No funds may be disbursed from the Treasury without an appropriation. Working capital fund balances are defined as appropriations. If they weren't, they couldn't be spent. For revolving funds, which include all working capital funds and many other funds, the purposes for which their money may be spent are defined in the statutory charter that set up the fund. If a working capital fund is set up by Congress to perform accounting and finance services for government agencies, money in such a fund may not be used for another purpose—say, overhauling an aircraft. The bottom line: Revolving funds are subject to the purpose law just like those operations funded by direct appropriations.

## 33. What if I have a need for an item I'm prohibited from buying with my appropriation. May I send my money off to another agency that has no such prohibition and have that agency buy it for me?

An agency may not do indirectly what it may not do directly.[6] You can't do an end-run around the law. An agency may not use a contract, grant, or agreement to accomplish a purpose it could not accomplish by direct expenditure.

### 34. Our appropriation simply funds a series of programs. It isn't specific about what sorts of items we may purchase. How do we know what is authorized?

It is common for appropriations to fund specific programs. For example, the Department of the Interior receives a separate appropriation to carry out the *Payments in Lieu of Taxes Act* (PILT), 31 U.S.C. 6901-6904. In this case the appropriation, while specific in its intent to fund PILT, is insufficient for an agency to use for further guidance. So the agency would need to look beyond the appropriation language and examine the PILT statute to determine what expenditures are authorized to support that program.[7]

### 35. The previous chapter discussed the general versus specific rule and the pick and stick rule. Are these rules part of the purpose law domain?

They are directly related to this discussion of purpose, and they bear repeating. The general versus specific rule states that even an expenditure that might be reasonably related to a general appropriation may not be paid out of that appropriation if there is a more specific appropriation available to cover it.[8] Pick and stick says that when two appropriations are available for the same purpose, the agency must select which one to use and continue to use that appropriation for that purpose unless the agency advises Congress of its intent to change to the other appropriation.

## NECESSARY EXPENSE DOCTRINE

### 36. My agency gets a very general appropriation for "operating expenses," and it specifies only a few examples of specific purpose. How do we determine what is authorized under such an appropriation?

Almost every agency gets at least one such general appropriation. These are called "lump sum" appropriations. Congress is not required to, nor could it, specify every item of expenditure in the appropriations acts.

The spending agency has reasonable discretion in determining how to carry out the objects of the appropriation. This concept, known as the "necessary expense doctrine," is what gives an agency some amount of flexibility or "wiggle room" in determining what it may or may not purchase. A 1927 comptroller general decision stated this doctrine as follows:[9]

> It is a well-settled rule of statutory construction that where an appropriation is made for a particular object, by implication it confers authority to incur expenses which are necessary or proper or incident to the proper execution of the object, unless there is another appropriation which makes more specific provision for such expenditures, or unless they are prohibited by law, or unless it is manifestly evident from various precedent appropriations acts that Congress has specifically legislated for certain expense of the Government, creating the implication that such expenditures should not be incurred except by its express authority.

The meaning of the above sentence is not immediately obvious to anyone. The following discussion will break down the elements of the necessary expense doctrine and demonstrate its use.

The necessary expense doctrine is a combination of two closely related but slightly different concepts:[10]

1. An appropriation made for a specific object is available for expenses necessarily incident to accomplishing that object unless prohibited by law or otherwise provided for. For example, an appropriation to erect a monument at the birthplace of George Washington may also be used to construct a fence around the monument to protect it. Thus, expenses incidental to the basic object may be purchased with the same appropriation.
2. Appropriations, even for such broad categories as salaries, frequently use the term *necessary expenses*. As used in this context, the term refers to "current or running expenses of a miscellaneous character arising out of and directly related to the agency's work."

There is no precise formula for applying the necessary expense doctrine. Determinations must be made on a case-by-case basis. When applying the necessary expense doctrine, an expenditure may be justified after meeting a three-part test:[11]

1. The expenditure must bear a logical relationship to the appropriation to be charged. In other words, it must make a direct contribution to carrying out either a specific appropriation or an authorized agency function for which more general appropriations are available.
2. The expenditure must not be prohibited by law.
3. The expenditure must not be otherwise provided for. That is, it must not be an item that falls within the scope of some other appropriation or statutory funding scheme.

## 37. Can you elaborate on the first test for justifying an expenditure—logical relationship to the appropriation?

This is the test with the greatest amount of ambiguity and the one that generates most of the questions to GAO. The rule does not require that a given expenditure be "necessary" in the sense that the object of the appropriation could not be fulfilled without it. So "necessary" does not mean "critical." On the other hand, it has to be more than merely desirable or even important. An expenditure may not be justified merely because an agency official thinks it is a good idea, nor may it be justified simply because it is a practice engaged in by private business.[12]

What the expenditure must do is contribute to accomplishing the purposes of the appropriation the agency wishes to charge. Agencies are granted a large degree of discretion in making the determination that an expenditure furthers the purposes of the appropriation. But this discretion is not unlimited. The determination must be reasonable and must be based on a permissible interpretation of the statute.[13]

An often referenced example of administrative discretion is the case of the marauding woodpeckers. In 1951, marauding woodpeckers were causing considerable damage to government-owned transmission lines, and the Southwestern Power Administration of the Department of the Interior wanted to buy guns with which to shoot the woodpeckers. Interior asked GAO if this was permissible. The comptroller general held that, if administratively determined to be necessary to protect the transmission lines, Interior could buy the guns and ammunition from the Southwestern Power Administration's construction appropriation. The views of the woodpeckers were not solicited.[14]

## 38. The second test for justifying an expenditure—must not be prohibited by law—seems fairly obvious. Can you give an example?

The Air Force asked GAO whether it could use its appropriation to install and maintain water pipelines carrying recycled storm and waste water to support a military base golf course. The idea was to support water conservation efforts in a dry, southwestern location. The comptroller general ruled that such use of their appropriation was not permissible because 10 U.S.C. 2246 specifically prohibits the use of appropriated funds to "equip, operate, or maintain" a golf course.[15] Thus, the desirability to participate in water conservation efforts by recycling water does not overcome a specific statutory prohibition.

## 39. The third test for justifying an expenditure—not otherwise provided for—sounds like a restatement of the specific versus general rule on the use of appropriation, wherein a more general appropriation may not be used for an object if a more specific appropriation is available for that purpose. Is that a correct interpretation?

Yes, it is. Even if the agency can make a logical case for using a particular appropriation for an expenditure, such a payment would be improper if the expenditure falls within the scope of another appropriation. The rule applies even if the more specific appropriation belongs to some other agency or if the proper appropriation is exhausted.

In 1959 the Navy could not use its shipbuilding appropriation to dredge a channel in the Singing River in Pascagoula, Mississippi, to permit submarines under construction to move to deep water in the Gulf of Mexico.[16] River dredging is a function for which the Corps of Engineers, not the Navy, receives an appropriation from Congress. Two facts of the case: (1) The appropriation to dredge rivers comes from a different appropriations act (Energy and Water Development) than the act by which the Navy is funded (Defense), and (2) no funds were available in the river dredging appropriation for the Singing River project. Both facts were irrelevant.

## SPECIFIC CATEGORIES OF EXPENDITURES—THE RULES

The remainder of this chapter explores the questions most commonly asked about various categories of expenses. Each category has a general rule about its use, as well as one or more exceptions. The objective is to describe what is authorized, the limitations or restrictions of that authorization, and what is not authorized. Refer to GAO's *Principles of Federal Appropriations Law*, Chapter 4, for additional information on expenses included in this book, as well as other kinds of expenses addressed by GAO but not included here because of a determination that they were not of common interest to most readers.

### *Training*

#### 40. Is there specific statutory authority to use federal funds to conduct training?

Training of government employees is governed by the *Government Employees Training Act* found in Title 5 of the *United States Code*.[17] Military members' training is governed by Title 10. Both titles specify what constitutes training under the statute and authorize the expenditure of government funds for training, both on a contractual basis and by using in-house resources.

Training of nonfederal personnel, where necessary to implement a federal program, is a "necessary expense" question under the relevant program appropriation.[18] It is possible to train contractors under the necessary expense doctrine. Agencies are warned to ensure that providing such training to contractors does not conflict with existing contractual language.

## *Travel*

### 41. Does reimbursement for travel expenses have a statutory basis?

Reimbursement for travel expenses incurred on official travel is authorized by statute (5 U.S.C. 5702). Agency discretion is broad, bounded only by the requirement that expenses are reimbursable to the extent authorized by statute and implementing regulations.[19]

### 42. May appropriated funds be used for officials' travel for political purposes?

To the extent it is possible to determine that a trip is for political purposes, the answer is "No"— appropriated funds should not be used for political travel. The Justice Department has observed it is often impossible to neatly categorize travel as purely business or purely political.[20] GAO on occasion has conducted reviews in this area and has commented on the lack of legally binding guidelines in this area. Agencies need to be careful in this area because even the perception that business travel (funded by appropriations) was done for political purposes can create controversy in the media or Congress.

## *Books and Periodicals*

### 43. What is the authority for purchasing books and periodicals?

Expenditures for books and periodicals are evaluated under the necessary expense doctrine. Agencies have broad discretion. For example, the Department of the Interior determined that subscribing to the *Federal Employees News Digest* was necessary in carrying out the agency's statutory functions.[21] Discretion is limited, however. The fact that a director, an avid golfer, wants a subscription to *Golf Digest* does not make it an authorized expenditure (unless, of course, the agency's mission includes golf).

## Charities and Civic Programs

### 44. May appropriated funds be used to support charities or civic programs (such as adopt-a-school programs)?

Agencies may spend their appropriations, within reason, to cooperate with government-sanctioned fund-raising campaigns, including such things as permitting solicitations during working hours, preparing and printing campaign instructions, and distributing campaign materials.[22] Also, some use of employee time and agency equipment may occur to assist with adopt-a-school programs.[23] The authority does not extend, however, to buying T-shirts to be given to each Combined Federal Campaign contributor. Such T-shirts were considered unauthorized gifts. Items may be purchased to "stimulate interest" in the campaign, but not as rewards for contributions.

## Meetings

### 45. May appropriated funds be used to send government employees to meetings?

The answer to this rather simple question is quite complicated. Let's begin by defining the word *meeting*. For our discussion the term includes such descriptions as conference, congress, convention, seminar, symposium, and workshop.[24] Generally speaking, a meeting occurs when two or more people convene for interaction on a particular matter. What we call such a gathering is irrelevant; for our purposes, they are all "meetings."

We start with federally sponsored meetings. When a federal agency sponsors a meeting, it normally does so under the necessary expense doctrine. Consequently, the travel, salaries, and expenses of government employees attending such a meeting are also authorized as necessary expenses. So-called "staff retreats" are becoming more common. So long as an agency official with the authority to do so determines that the retreat is a necessary expense, it is an authorized and legal expense of the agency exercising its administrative discretion. Although such retreats might at times be criticized as wasteful or extravagant, they are not inherently illegal.[25]

Now we turn the discussion to meetings that are not federally sponsored. A law passed in 1912, still on the books and found at 5 U.S.C. 5946, prohibits the use of appropriated funds to pay the expenses of attendance at meetings or conventions of members of a society or association. GAO consistently disallowed expenses for attendance at any such meeting of societies or associations.[26] Then, in 1958, Congress passes the *Government Employees Training Act*, which includes two provisions that apply to meetings. 5 U.S.C. 4109 authorizes payment of expenses in connection with authorized training. 5 U.S.C. 4110 authorizes expenses for meetings "which are concerned with the functions or activities for which the appropriation is made or which will contribute to improved conduct, supervision, or management of the functions or activities."[27]

With the above discussion completed, it is possible to summarize the rules.

1. Government employees may attend a federally sponsored meeting at government expense.
2. Government employees may attend a non-federally sponsored meeting at government expense if:
    a. It is part of an authorized training program under 5 U.S.C. 4109, or
    b. It is related to agency functions or management under 5 U.S.C. 4110.
3. If neither 5 U.S.C. 4109 nor 5 U.S.C. 4110 applies, and the meeting is a meeting of a "society or association," then the prohibition of 5 U.S.C. 5946 applies and expenses may not be paid from government funds.[28]

## 46. May appropriated funds be used to pay the meeting expenses of non-federal personnel?

In 1935 Congress passed a statute, now found at 31 U.S.C. 1345, that states:

> Except as specifically provided by law, an appropriation may not be used for travel, transportation, and subsistence expenses for a meeting. This section does not prohibit—

> (1) an agency from paying the expenses of an officer or employee of the United States Government carrying out an official duty; . . . .[29]

Clearly this law was aimed at using government funds to pay the expenses of non-federal people. Although GAO has not attempted to define exactly what sort of activities qualify as a "meeting" under the law and makes its determinations on a case-by-case basis, GAO has consistently denied expenses in matters brought to its attention by interpreting the statutory language quite broadly. Examples where payment was denied include:[30]

- The U.S. Environmental Protection Agency was not authorized to pay for state officials to attend a National Solid Waste Management Association Convention.
- The Mine Safety and Health Administration was not allowed to pay for miners and mine operators attending safety and health training.
- The National Highway Traffic Safety Administration could not pay the expenses of state officials at a workshop on odometer fraud.

Note that although an agency may have the authority to put on a meeting, such as those listed above, such authority is not sufficient to pay the expenses of attendance for non-federal personnel. Thus, an agency may rent a room, hire speakers, and pay for its own personnel to attend, but the non-federal attendees are on their own to finance their attendance.

## 47. Suppose an agency wants to have a non-federal person speak at a federally sponsored meeting. May the agency pay travel expenses in that instance?

Yes. Another statute, enacted in 1946 and found at 5 U.S.C. 5703, applies to the so-called "invitational travel" situation, wherein a private party is called upon by the government to confer or advise on government business. This represents a limited exception to the prohibition against paying expenses for non-federal personnel. A critical prerequisite, however, is that the person must be performing a direct service to the government.[31] Thus, making a presentation at a meeting suffices.

The exception does not apply when there is only an indirect benefit to the government, as in the previously cited example of state environmental officials attending a federal meeting on waste management. Although there certainly might be some real benefits to the government in having the state officials attend, the invitational travel exception did not apply because the state officials were providing no direct service to the government at the meeting.

### 48. My agency administers grant funds, and our grantees often sponsor meetings and pay for non-federal personnel to attend. Are they violating the prohibition found in 5 U.S.C. 1345?

Once a grant has been made for an authorized grant purpose, the funds now in the hands of the grantee are not subject to many of the restrictions that apply to the direct expenditure of appropriations. This is the case for 31 U.S.C. 1345, which does not apply to grant funds in the hands of a grantee.[32] Thus, grantees may use such grant funds to pay expenses for attendance at meetings by non-federal personnel.

However, an agency may not use the grant mechanism for the sole purpose of circumventing 31 U.S.C. 1345, that is, to do indirectly that which it could not do directly. Thus, an agency may not make a grant for the express purpose of sponsoring a conference at which non-federals attendance would be paid for.[33]

## *Entertainment*

### 49. Are appropriated funds available to pay for entertainment?

The general rule is that appropriated funds may not be used for entertainment except when specifically authorized by statute and also authorized or approved by proper administrative officers. The basis for this rule is that entertainment is a personal expense, even when it occurs in some business-related context. Entertainment cannot normally be said to be necessary to carry out the purposes of the appropriation.[34]

## 50. Entertainment is considered a legitimate business expense in the private sector. Can't the same rationale be applied in a government setting?

Clearly there is a different standard for government funds. GAO summarized this difference in B-223678, June 5, 1989:

> The theory is not so much that these items can never be business-related, because sometimes they clearly are. Rather, what the decisions are really saying is that, because public confidence in the integrity of those who spend the taxpayers' money is essential, certain items which may appear frivolous or wasteful – however legitimate they may in fact be in a specific context – should, if they are to be charged to public funds, be authorized specifically by the Congress.[35]

B-2888266, January 27, 2003, puts it another way:

> Reference to "common business practice" is not in itself an adequate justification for spending public money on food, or for that matter, other objects. An expenditure of public funds must be anchored in existing law, not the practices and conventions of the private sector.[36]

## 51. The term *entertainment* is quite broad. What sorts of objects are included in its definition?

GAO has not precisely defined the term *entertainment*. However, various courts and comptroller general decisions have given several examples that indicate its meaning. Following are examples of entertainment:[37]

- Source or means of amusement, a diverting performance, as a concert, drama, or the like
- A pleasurable occupation of the senses
- Dancing, sports, or music
- Food and drink, either formal meals or snacks or refreshments
- Receptions, banquets and the like

- Music, live or recorded
- Live artistic performances
- Recreational facilities
- Liquor
- Cocktail parties, banquets and dinners, theater attendance, sightseeing parties.

These examples cut a wide swath. A good rule of thumb: If there is any question about whether a particular expense is entertainment, it probably is not.

## 52. Buying food with appropriated funds is an ongoing debate in my agency. What is the rule on buying food, and what are the exceptions?

The general rule is that appropriated funds may not be used to provide free food to government employees at their official duty stations, unless specifically authorized by law. Food is a personal expense, and government salaries are presumed adequate to enable employees to eat regularly. The prohibition applies to snacks and refreshments (including coffee) as well as meals.[38]

There are exceptions:

- Meals of employees in travel status
- Employees working in emergency situations
- *Government Employees Training Act*
- *Government Employees Incentive Awards Act*
- Cultural awareness programs
- Necessary expense of carrying out the agency mission.

## 53. Can you elaborate on each of the exceptions to the rule on buying food?

**Employees in travel status**. There is specific statutory authority to reimburse employees for meals when they are in travel status. One must remember, however, that being in a travel status involves two components—distance and time. The employee must have traveled outside the area defined by the agency as the official duty station, and the travel must have exceeded 12 hours. If the distance and time criteria are not both met, the employee is considered to be "at the duty station" and food would not be authorized. Traveling across town to a conference at a local hotel would not put the employee in travel status.

**Employees working in emergency situations**. This is a very limited exception that agencies often try to stretch to include working under unusual or extreme conditions. Examples where reimbursement has been denied include:[39]

- Federal mediators required to conduct mediation sessions after regular hours
- District of Columbia police officers involved in cleanup work after a fire
- Inspectors at offshore oil rigs who had few alternatives to buying lunch from private caterers at excessive prices
- Law enforcement personnel retained at staging areas for security purposes prior to being dispatched to execute search warrants.

The exception applies to situations where there is an emergency that involves imminent danger to human life or the destruction of federal property. One example was a cadre of General Services Administration (GSA) police who spent the night in alert status at a building that had been occupied by unauthorized individuals. Sandwiches and coffee for the security personnel were considered incidental to the protection of government property during this emergency that involved danger to human life and the destruction of federal property.[40] The exception is limited, however. Merely being required to remain on duty for a 24-hour period is not enough. Dangerous conditions are not enough. Finally, inclement weather that does not rise to the level of an emergency situation does not support an exception to the rule.

***Government Employees Training Act***. The Act authorizes agencies to pay for the necessary expenses of training as well as expenses for attendance at meetings that are concerned with the functions or activities for which the appropriation is made. The comptroller general has issued decisions that provide for paying the costs of meals and refreshments at meetings and training events under specific circumstances.[41]

1. Attendance at meeting and conferences[42]

    a. For day-to-day routine agency-sponsored business meetings, the Training Act does ***not*** provide authority to use appropriations to supply food items. Day-to-day business meetings are those that involve discussions of the internal procedures or operations of the agency.

    b. For meetings sponsored by nongovernment organizations, attendees are often charged a fee, usually called a registration fee. If a single fee covers both attendance and meals, and no separate charge is made for meals, the government may pay the full fee. This could extend to an evening social event where the cost is a mandatory, nonseparable element of the registration fee.

    c. If the meeting sponsor makes a separate charge for meals, the government may pay for the meals if the agency can show all of the following:

        (1) The meals are incidental to the meeting.

        (2) Attendance of the employee at the meals is necessary to full participation in the business of the conference.

        (3) The employee is not free to take the meals elsewhere without being absent from essential formal discussions, lectures, or speeches concerning the purpose of the conference.

2. Training[43]

    When real training, as defined by the *Government Employees Training Act*, occurs, the government may pay or reimburse for necessary expenses incident to the training. This rule applies whether the training is sponsored by a nongovernmental organization or the government itself. As with meetings, an agency may pay for the cost of meals and refreshments if they are included as an incidental and nonseparable portion of a training or attendance fee. If the cost of the food is not included in a registration or attendance fee, the government may provide meals or refreshments if the agency determines that providing such food is necessary to achieve the objectives of the training program. The government may also furnish meals to nongovernment speakers as an expense of conducting the training.

**Award ceremonies.**[44] Appropriations may be used to provide meals or refreshments at award ceremonies under the *Government Employees Incentive Awards Act*. It is important to note that the ceremony must include public recognition of the award recipients in order to qualify for the providing of meals or refreshments. Further, although it is possible to combine an awards ceremony with a social event, say, a dance or picnic, agencies must be cautious because such expenditures would be subject to greater scrutiny than expenditures made in connection with more traditional awards ceremonies.

**Cultural awareness programs.**[45] Small samples of ethnic foods served during a formal ethnic awareness program as part of an agency's equal employment opportunity program may be purchased with appropriated funds. These tidbits must be true "samples" and not rise to the level of refreshments or meals.

**Necessary expense to carry out the agency mission**. Examples of this exception are rare. It is difficult to imagine many scenarios where an agency must provide food to an employee in order to carry out its mission. One example would be a human research laboratory studying the effects of various foods or liquor on employee performance. To test the effect of alcohol on reaction time of an airplane pilot, it might be necessary to purchase a supply of vodka, which the pilot would consume during a study. Such a situation would meet the tests of the necessary expense doctrine and be an authorized expenditure.

## 54. What about entertainment for government personnel that does not involve food? Is that an authorized expenditure?

There are very few decisions in this area, presumably because there are very few situations where such entertainment could conceivably be authorized.[46] One exception is the previously mentioned cultural awareness programs. In addition to providing food samples, such cultural awareness programs, which are designed to further the agency's equal opportunity program, may include live artistic performances, such as dance troupes or singers. An agency may expend appropriated funds for such entertainment, so long as the planned performances advance Equal Employment Opportunity objectives.

## 55. If we can't normally use appropriated funds for entertaining government employees, does it follow that entertaining nongovernment personnel is also prohibited?

Correct. The basic rule is the same regardless of who is being entertained. Appropriated funds are not available for entertainment, including food, except under specific statutory authority.[47]

The Department of Veterans Affairs justified the purchase of refreshments for nongovernment employees—veterans—using the necessary expense doctrine. GAO agreed that the VA could purchase refreshments as an incentive to get veterans to attend focus groups where the agency satisfies its legislative mandate to measure and evaluate its programs.[48] Because the refreshments increased participation in the focus groups, the quality of the information gathered by the VA was improved.

## 56. One subject not mentioned yet is Official Representation Funds. Can't these funds be used for entertainment, including food?

The rule we've been looking at says that government funds may not be used for entertainment, *unless specifically authorized by law*. Congress recognizes that many agencies have a legitimate need for items that would otherwise be prohibited as entertainment, and responds by making limited amounts of funds available for official entertainment.[49]

Entertainment appropriations take many forms and have various names. The names include Reception and Representation Funds, Official Representation Funds, Representation Allowances, and Protocol Funds; the Department of Defense (DoD) receives earmarks in its Operation and Maintenance appropriations for Emergencies and Extraordinary Expenses. These appropriations may take the form of permanent, indefinite appropriations; annual or multiyear appropriations; no-year appropriations; or earmarks within an agency's fixed-term appropriations.

Unless specifically bound by appropriation language, agencies have wide discretion in the use of their Reception and Representation funds. There must be some connection with official agency business,[50] but having satisfied that criterion, the agency determines how it will administer its R&R funds. Because these funds are very limited, agencies typically place strong internal controls on their use, and approvals are kept at a high level within the agency.

## 57. This discussion on food has been very complex. Is there a way to summarize what agencies are and are not allowed to buy with appropriated funds?

GAO created a decision tree that simplifies the analysis process considerably. You can find it at Appendix 1 of this book. When using the decision tree, make sure you carefully read the cited decision to ensure it applies to your particular situation.

## 58. Although agencies may not generally purchase food for employees, may they use appropriated funds to purchase equipment to cook or store food? This would include such items as coffee makers, refrigerators, and microwaves.

GAO has allowed such purchases in some instances. When the agency has determined that providing such equipment and facilities is significant in hiring and retaining employees, it has been allowed. Likewise, when no eating facilities are readily available due to distance, 24-hour operations, or security concerns, GAO has allowed refrigerators and microwaves.

In 2004 GAO retreated from its previous stance that such items are generally personal in nature and left it up to agencies to justify their purchase under the necessary expense doctrine. GAO recognized that the workplace has changed over time and such food-related equipment is common in many workplaces. If agencies demonstrate that providing such equipment is reasonably related to efficient performance of agency activities and provides other benefits, such as a safer workplace, agencies may justify the use of appropriated funds. GAO made it clear that such equipment needs to be in a common area available for use by all personnel and that the cost of food items and coffee remained personal expenses that fall upon each employee.[51]

## *Child Care and Elder Care*

### 59. Some agencies provide child care facilities or subsidize child care. Do employees have an entitlement to receiving such child care support?

Employees do not have an entitlement to child care at government expense. Under the necessary expense doctrine, an agency may provide child care support when it has determined that such expenditures would contribute materially to recruitment, retention, morale, and hence efficiency and effectiveness.

In 1985 Congress enacted legislation that authorizes, but does not require, federal agencies to provide space and services for child care centers. The term *services* includes utilities, equipment, appliances, and security systems. Space and services may be provided with or without charge.[52]

Congress provided permanent authority in 2001 for agencies to use appropriated funds "to improve the affordability of child care for lower income Federal employees."[53] The Office of Personnel Management has issued regulations governing such support to lower income employees (5 CFR 792).

### 60. If appropriated fund support is available for child care, what about elder care?

So far, GAO has ruled that elder care is not a necessary expense and agency appropriations are not available for such costs. As previously mentioned, Congress has authorized support for child care. GAO has opined that it was "for the Congress to decide whether agency appropriations could be used to support eldercare centers."[54]

As demographics change and the need for elder care increases over time, expect this topic to be revisited by the Congress and GAO in the future.

## *Fines and Penalties*

### 61. I inadvertently parked a government vehicle in a "No Parking" zone. I returned just as a policeman was finishing the ticket. My agency refused to reimburse me for the cost of the ticket even though I was operating the vehicle for official business. Why wasn't I reimbursed?

Generally speaking, an agency may not use appropriated funds to pay fines and penalties assessed against its employees.[55] Employees are expected to comply with the law in carrying out their duties. Violating laws, even parking laws, is outside the scope of their employment, and employees must therefore take personal responsibility for any resulting liability.

One exception is when the agency determines that paying a fine or penalty levied on an employee is a necessary expense. In the case of *Sam Giancana v. J. Edgar Hoover*, an FBI agent had been instructed by the agency to refuse to testify and was fined for contempt of court. In this case there was a legitimate government interest in his compliance with the instructions not to testify. Because he was without fault in incurring the fine, the FBI could reimburse him under the necessary expense doctrine.[56]

### 62. If a fine or penalty is levied directly on a federal agency, may the agency pay it?

Under the concept of sovereign immunity, the general answer is "No." Sovereign immunity would need to be waived by statute for such an expenditure to be authorized.[57]

One example of such a waiver is the *Clean Air Act*. It makes federal agencies liable for violation of the Act, and paying state and locally imposed civil penalties for such violation is therefore authorized.[58]

## 63. Do federal agencies pay fines or penalties levied by other federal agencies, for example, by the Internal Revenue Service?

Absent specific statutory authority, federal agencies may not use their appropriated funds to pay fines or penalties to other federal entities.[59]

### *Gifts and Awards*

## 64. What is the difference between a gift and an award?

An award is something given in recognition of previous accomplishments, and usually with the expectation of future positive accomplishments benefiting the agency. Thus, an award involves a give and take, with government benefit part of the "taking." A gift involves no such give and take. A gift is not based on prior accomplishment and has no expectation of future actions.

## 65. May an agency buy gifts for employees or members of the public?

Without specific statutory authority, agencies may not purchase personal gifts with appropriated funds.[60] Exceptions to this general statement all involve some government benefit from the purchase of what otherwise seem to be personal gifts. Given the large sums of money agencies have available, the potential for abuse is enormous. Therefore, GAO has taken a very strict approach in its decisions on gifts. There are more decisions where the purchase of gifts has been denied than where it has been approved.

## 66. What are some of the exceptions on gift giving?

One exception is gifts used as recruiting tools. For example, an item of nominal value, such as a pen or refrigerator magnet containing a phone number or website address, might be an effective way of providing potential employees with information they need to contact the agency should they be interested in employment.[61] However, items without such contact information have been determined to be nothing more than "favorable reminders" of the agency that did not facilitate recruiting efforts.[62]

Agencies involved in direct sales to the public might also be able to give something to customers to compensate them for previous poor service. GAO found that the U.S. Mint could give complimentary commemorative coins to customers whose orders the mint had mishandled. This goodwill gesture of giving the complimentary coins would contribute to the success of the Mint's commemorative sales program.[63]

Another exception is when the gift is purely informational and has no intrinsic value to the recipients. For example, buttons or magnets inscribed with messages related to agency programs would fall into this category.[64] Such items benefit the agency, not the employee, by disseminating agency information.

A memento, such as a plaque to a guest speaker, would also be allowable. The government received the benefit of the guest speaker's message, and a nominal gift is an appropriate gesture of thanks for their services. The speaker ought not be a government employee or anyone being paid under contract, however.

## 67. What about awards? May an agency use its appropriated funds to award its employees or others?

The *Government Employees Incentives Awards Act* allows agencies to award employees for their "suggestion, invention, superior accomplishment, or other personal effort" that contributes to the efficiency and effectiveness of government operations. Under the Act, agencies may also incur necessary expenses associated with issuing such incentive awards.[65]

## 68. Under the *Government Employees Incentive Awards Act*, what forms may the awards take?

Awards may be in the form of cash, time off, or merchandise. Among the merchandise items found allowable are the following:[66]

- Plaques
- Jackets

- Coffee mugs
- Tickets to sporting events and amusement parks
- Meals or gift certificates for meals.

Remember, however, that awards must be based upon an act or service related to official employment.

## 69. Are length of service or retirement awards authorized?

Cash awards for length of service or retirement are not authorized. Honorary noncash awards are permissible.[67]

## 70. We have an employee who hasn't used any sick leave in the past ten years. May the agency give him an award under the Act?

GAO has ruled that the use of incentive awards for good sick leave usage is inappropriate.[68] The employee has already been compensated by having a large sick leave balance available should it be needed in the future.

## 71. Several contractors work in our office on a continuous basis. Our agency has Teamwork Awards that often include such contractors. May the contractors receive the same awards as the government employees on the team?

Remember the law is called the *Government Employees Incentives Awards Act*. It does not apply to contractors, nor does it apply to state or local government officials who might be involved with a federal program.[69] Such personnel are not authorized to receive cash or merchandise under the Act. Publicly recognizing such personnel along with the government employees, and providing a letter or certificate to them, is about as far as an agency may go.

## 72. In a previous answer there was mention of "necessary expenses associated with issuing such incentive awards." Of what might those expenses consist?

One such associated expense would be travel of the employee to the location where the award is to be presented. Agencies may also pay the travel expenses for those accompanying the employee to the ceremony. Also allowable are the travel expenses of someone receiving the award on behalf of a deceased recipient.[70]

Another necessary expense is the cost of the incentive awards ceremony itself. As mentioned previously under the "food" section, such ceremonies may include refreshments.[71] Other expenses of the ceremony might include rental of a facility and flowers or other decorations.

Remember that simply distributing one or more awards in conjunction with an event or function designed to achieve other objectives does not make it an awards ceremony where refreshments would be authorized. The underlying purpose of the event must be awards, and the refreshments must facilitate public recognition of the award recipients. Agencies are given considerable discretion in carrying out their awards programs, but that discretion is not unlimited.

### *Insurance*

## 73. I've heard that the federal government is self-insured—that it doesn't buy insurance. Is that true?

Generally speaking, yes. The rule is that unless there is specific statutory authority, appropriated funds are not available for the purchase of insurance to cover loss or damage to government employees or the liability of government employees.[72]

## 74. What is the rationale for the government's policy on insurance?

There are two basic aspects. First, the federal government has more money (or at least, access to more money through its taxing authority) than anyone else. It has more money than all the insurance companies put together. Thus, if it wrecks a government-owned car, it just buys another one. Second, given the amount of government resources available, it doesn't make sense to purchase private insurance, which would include amounts for operating expenses, overhead, and the company's profits. It is more economical for the government to insure itself against loss.[73]

## 75. Are there exceptions to the rule regarding insurance?

Of course there are. For example, the government contributes to the cost of health and life insurance under the Federal Employees' Health Benefits Program and the Federal Employees' Group Life Insurance. Agencies are also required by statute to pay half of the cost incurred by qualified employees for professional liability insurance. Also, in the course of paying for contracts, grants, and leases, the government is paying for insurance that is indirectly passed on by vendors and grantees as a cost of doing business.[74]

Congress may also specifically authorize the purchase of insurance in certain cases. Even in those cases, the agency normally has the discretion to purchase, or not purchase, the insurance.

In addition, there are nonstatutory exceptions where the underlying policy considerations do not apply. These are summarized by GAO as follows:[75]

- Where the economy sought by self-insurance would be defeated
- Where sound business practice indicates that a savings can be effected
- Where services or benefits not otherwise available can be obtained by purchasing insurance.

Insurance is occasionally purchased as an incidental expense of purchasing some other authorized object. For example, travel agents who charge the government a flat fee for issuing airline tickets often include some level of free flight insurance as part of their service. The cost of the flight insurance is not priced separately. Thus, the flight insurance is incidental to the purchase of the plane ticket, and the government has paid for it in the course of having the ticket issued. However, the government may not pay for flight insurance when it must be purchased separately, for example on non-ticketed flights taken by National Transportation Safety Board employees investigating accidents. Flight insurance is considered a personal expense.[76]

## 76. May an agency pay for insurance, or a surety bond, to cover employees who handle cash or other valuables?

In 1972 Congress passed legislation specifically prohibiting the government from requiring or paying for surety bonds for civilian employees or military members in conjunction with the performance of their official duties. The purpose of the legislation was to observe the aims of the self-insurance rule and to substitute the practice of self-insurance for the previous practice of obtaining surety bonds on such employees.[77]

### *Memberships and Dues*

## 77. I belong to a professional association that is related to my government job. May my agency pay the annual membership dues?

No. A 1912 prohibits the use of appropriated funds to pay membership fees of an employee in a society or association.[78]

## 78. My association offers discounts on training to members that would exceed the cost of the membership. Given the economies to be had, could the agency buy the membership using cost savings as a justification?

No. Regardless of the resulting benefit to the agency, membership fees for individuals may not be paid.[79] An agency may purchase a membership in the name of the agency, however, if doing so would let the agency receive the reduced cost as a benefit of membership.[80]

## 79. My agency has appointed me as its national representative to the Federally Employed Women program. Since this is directly related to my job, can the agency pay my annual membership fee to FEW, Inc.?

GAO has ruled that the fact the membership is job-related does not overcome the statutory prohibition.[81] So the agency may not pay your dues.

## 80. Are there any exceptions to the prohibition against paying for individual memberships?

Other than an appropriation specifically passed for that purpose, the only exception is under the *Government Employees Training Act*. If the agency determines that training from a particular membership organization for an employee is required, and if that organization requires individual membership to receive such training, then the agency could pay for the membership as a necessary expense of obtaining the required training.[82] Public speaking training through Toastmasters International is an example.

### *Business Cards*

## 81. What is the rule on the purchase of business cards?

As a general rule, business cards are considered personal expenses and government funds are not available for their purchase. However, the agency may, using the "necessary expense" analysis, determine that such purchase is allowable for employees who regularly deal with the public or organizations outside their immediate office.[83] Recruiters and customer service representatives are among the employees who would fall within this exception.

### *Medical Care and Health-Related Items*

## 82. May an agency provide medical care to employees using appropriated funds?

Except for illness directly resulting from the nature of the employment, medical care is considered a personal expense and government funds may not be used.[84]

Some further exceptions have been granted when the expense primarily benefited the government, rather than the employee. These involved physical examinations and inoculations.[85]

In addition, an agency is authorized to establish and run health service programs to promote and maintain the physical and mental fitness of its employees. Such authorized health service programs are limited to:[86]

- Treatment of on-the-job illness and dental conditions requiring emergency attention
- Pre-employment and other examinations
- Referral of employees to private physicians and dentists
- Preventive programs relating to health.

Thus, the government may pay for smoking cessation classes but not for the treatment of any medical problems associated with a person's smoking habit.

## 83. What about health-related items, such as prescription eyeglasses? May appropriated funds be used for those?

Health-related items are considered personal equipment and therefore personal expenses.[87] If an employee needs prescription eyeglasses to perform the job, the employee is expected to provide them.

However, there are exceptions. For example, if the employee works in a machine shop running a metal lathe, *Occupational Safety and Health Act* standards would apply and the purchase of prescription safety goggles would be authorized.[88]

In addition, the *Rehabilitation Act of 1973** applies to federal agencies. "Reasonable accommodations" for employees with disabilities are required and could include health-related items.[89]

* The *Rehabilitation Act* is related to the better-known *Americans with Disabilities Act*. The *Americans with Disabilities Act* does not apply to federal employers, but its standards are used to determine compliance with the *Rehabilitation Act*, which does apply to federal employers.

## *Office Decorations*

### 84. Appropriations are obviously available to purchase office furnishings such as tables and chairs. But what about office decorations that serve no real utilitarian purpose?

This is a "necessary expense" question. Agencies may determine that office decorations are necessary for the public purpose. Such decorations may take the form of pictures, art objects, plants, flowers (both real and artificial), and similar items. Purchases must be justified because they enhance the morale or productivity of the organization, not because they are for the personal convenience or desire of a given employee.[90]

### 85. Would the same rule apply to seasonal decorations such as pumpkins, trees, lights, and ornaments?

Yes. In 1987 GAO concluded that the rule for office decorations is the same whether the decorations are permanent or temporary.[91] However, agencies need to be sensitive with respect to the display of religious symbols. Agencies buying such seasonal decorations should closely review B-226011, B-226900, November 17, 1987 (one decision) before proceeding.

## *Greeting Cards*

### 86. If seasonal decorations are authorized, then what about seasonal greeting cards?

GAO has made a clear distinction between seasonal decorations and greeting cards. Such greeting cards, even those that are "agency to agency," are not authorized to be purchased from government funds. Likewise, GAO has found that seasonal or holiday "letters" are also not authorized to be produced or mailed at government expense.[92]

## Ceremonial Items

### 87. What about such items as ribbons and scissors for a ribbon-cutting ceremony or champagne for launching a ship?

Agencies may purchase items associated with such traditional ceremonies. In addition to ribbon, scissors, and champagne (to break on the hull, not for the reception afterwards), engraved and chrome-plated shovels for a ground-breaking ceremony, and flowers and printed invitations for such ceremonies are allowable.[93]

## Certifications and Licenses

### 88. May an agency pay for certifications, licenses, and examinations necessary to obtain such certifications or licenses?

Historically, employees were always expected to bear the expense of qualifying themselves for their position. Thus, government funds were not generally available for such personal qualification expenses. In 2001, however, Congress enacted legislation permitting agencies to use appropriated funds for such expenses. These may include state-imposed and professional licenses, expenses for professional accreditation and professional certification, and examinations to obtain such credentials. The statute did not create an entitlement; agencies use their discretion to determine whether to pay for such expenses.[94]

### 89. Does the law concerning personal qualification expenses cover driver's licenses?

That is unclear. If an agency wants to use the 2001 law as its authority to pay for an employee's driver's license, the agency would have to classify the license as a professional credential, professional accreditation, state-imposed and professional license, or professional certification.[95] Failing that, the agency would have to fall back on the necessary expense doctrine to justify the expense. In such cases the license would need to benefit the agency, rather than the employee. One could likely make a case that purchase of an International Driver's License (IDL) for employees traveling to countries requiring the IDL in addition to a state-issued license is a necessary expense. Renewal of an employee's state-issued license, on the other hand, doesn't seem to meet the necessary expense criteria.

## *Clothing*

### 90. Employee clothing appears to be a personal expense. When may the government pay for clothing?

Let's start with the general rule and work from there. The general rule is that "every employee of the Government is required to present himself for duty properly attired according to the requirements of his position."[96]

Keeping that general rule in mind, we then ask the question: Is the employee unable to perform the job satisfactorily without the proposed piece of clothing or equipment? This is another way of asking: Is the item "necessary"? If the answer is "no," the employee is expected to furnish the item because any benefit accrues to the employee, not the government.

If the answer is "yes," the follow-up question is: Is it reasonable to require the employee to furnish the item? Criteria for answering this question include whether the item is to be used by the employee in connection with his regular duties or only in emergencies or at infrequent intervals, and whether the item is assigned to an employee for individual use or is intended for and actually to be used by different employees. If it is reasonable to require the employee to furnish the item, the government doesn't pay for it. If it is not reasonable, the government may buy it but retains ownership of the item.[97]

### 91. Are there specific statutes that allow the purchase of wearing apparel?

There are three general statutory provisions that allow agencies to purchase such items, in certain limited circumstances.

First is the *Administrative Expenses Act of 1946*. To satisfy this statute, three tests must be met:[98]

1. The item must be "special" and not part of the ordinary and usual furnishings an employee would reasonably be expected to provide.
2. The item must be for the benefit of the government—essential to the safe and successful accomplishment of the work and not solely for the protection of the employee.
3. The employee must be engaged in hazardous duty.

Second is the *Occupational Safety and Health Act of 1970* (OSHA). An agency may furnish protective clothing if it determines that it is necessary under OSHA and its implementing regulations.[99]

Often, an item could be justified under either of these two statutes. Following are some examples where the purchase of clothing items was permissible:[100]

- Snowmobile gear for employees required to operate snowmobiles in remote forest areas
- Down-filled parkas for employees temporarily assigned to Alaska or the high country of western states
- Cooler coats and gloves for Department of Agriculture meat graders
- Steel-toed safety shoes for an employee required to move heavy objects.

Conversely, here are some examples that do not meet the criteria of either law, and purchase of the items is not allowed:[101]

- Rubber boots and coats for custodial employees in flood-prone areas
- Coats and gloves for government drivers
- Insulated coveralls for employees working outside in near-freezing temperatures
- Raincoats and umbrellas for employees who must frequently go out in the rain
- Coveralls for mechanics.

The third statute that allows for the purchase of wearing apparel is the *Federal Employees Uniform Act*. The Act authorizes agencies to prescribe uniforms for employees and either pay a cash allowance or furnish the uniform.[102] Some agencies have additional specific authority to prescribe and provide uniforms to their employees.

It is important to remember that a "uniform" is an item of distinctive design that allows an observer to identify the wearer as part of a particular group. Business suits, and even tuxedos, do not fit the definition. Calling a business suit a uniform doesn't make it one.

## *Commuting, Parking, and Flexiplace*

### 92. My agency moved its location across town, greatly increasing my commute to and from work. Further, there was ample free parking at the old location, but now I have to pay for parking at a commercial garage. May the agency pay for some or all of my commuting and parking expenses?

Employees are expected to get to work. How they do that is up to each employee, and the cost of doing so is considered a personal expense. So the cost of your commute, even though it is longer, cannot be reimbursed by your agency.[103]

Parking is also considered a personal expense. The government doesn't owe employees a parking spot. However, an agency may provide for parking if it is determined to be a necessary expense because the lack of parking will impair operating efficiency and be detrimental to the hiring and retention of personnel. Thus, the agency ***may*** provide parking even though it is not required to do so.[104]

### 93. Occasionally I'm called back to work in the evening after working my normal shift. Shouldn't the agency reimburse me for the second commute to and from work?

You are being compensated for the time you spend at work when called back. Commuting is commuting, whether it happens once, twice, or more times per day. So the agency may not reimburse you for these additional trips.[105]

## 94. Some of my co-workers ride mass transit to work and get a subsidy to help pay the cost. Isn't that a violation of the rule stated above?

It would be—except there is specific legislation that allows it. In 1993 Congress authorized agencies to establish programs to encourage the use of other than single-occupancy vehicles. The purpose is to reduce road congestion and improve air quality. Such programs may include transit passes or cash reimbursement for passes, the furnishing of space or services to bicyclists, and nonmonetary incentives. In 2000 Executive Order 13150 required agencies to implement a transportation fringe benefit program under the 1993 law.[106]

## 95. Flexiplace, or teleworking, is becoming more and more prevalent. What expenses may the agency pay for in relation to such work from home arrangements?

The agency may purchase and furnish equipment (computers, fax machines, etc.) and telephone and data lines and may pay monthly fees for such lines for an employee authorized to work from home. Equipment so furnished remains the property of the government.[107]

## 96. May I ask for reimbursement from my agency for the portion of my heating, air-conditioning, and lighting costs that reflects the amount of time I spend teleworking and the portion of my house where I work?

You can ask, but the agency won't pay. These are considered personal expenses and may not be reimbursed, absent specific statutory authority. Although you might suffer some additional utility costs, they are more than covered by reduced commuting, child care, meal, and/or clothing expenses. Even if the work at home arrangement is mandatory rather than voluntary, incremental costs of utilities associated with the residence may not be reimbursed.[108] However, additional out-of-pocket costs incurred making official long distance phone calls are reimbursable.

## *Motor Vehicles*

### 97. I've noticed that many appropriations contain specific authority to buy a given number of cars. Why is that?

Statutory controls over the acquisition and use of motor vehicles date back to 1914 with the enactment of what is now 31 U.S.C. 1343(b). The 1914 law required specific authority to use appropriated funds "for the purchase of any motor-propelled or horse-drawn passenger-carrying vehicle for the service of any of the executive departments or other Government establishments, or any branch of the Government service." The law was amended in 1946 to delete the reference to horses; to expand the prohibition to "purchase or hire;" and to exempt vehicles for the use of the President, secretaries to the President, or the heads of cabinet departments.[109] It also requires specific authority to use appropriations, other than those of the armed forces, to buy, maintain, or operate aircraft. In 1982 the word *hire* became *lease*. Thus, an agency may not use its appropriated funds to purchase or lease any passenger-carrying vehicle.

### 98. Can you provide examples of passenger-carrying vehicles?

Many decisions came out after this legislation was passed in 1914. Here are some examples of passenger-carrying vehicles subject to the restriction: sedans, limousines, station wagons, ambulances, and motorcycles.

Not governed by the law are trucks, jeeps, motor boats, and passenger automobiles used for testing.

The test is one of construction and design, rather than intended use. Even though a truck might be used to carry passengers, its design is for hauling cargo.[110] Therefore, the restriction does not apply.

## 99. How restrictive is the prohibition against leasing?

The prohibition against leasing was inserted to prevent agencies from dodging the prohibition against purchasing vehicles by merely leasing them. It does not apply to the rental of taxicabs or other vehicles on a "per trip" basis incident to normal day-to-day business. It also does not apply to the rental of vehicles by employees on official travel.[111]

### *Rewards*

## 100. May a government employee be paid a reward for providing information to capture someone who is wanted by the law?

It depends on the scope of the employee's duties. Consider the following examples:[112]

- A Deputy U.S. Marshall apprehended a military deserter. He could not be paid the reward because he had been acting in his official capacity (it was his job to capture deserters).
- A patrol inspector for the Immigration Service apprehended a military deserter. A reward was payable because he was acting in the capacity of a private citizen, outside the scope of his official duties.

### *Taxes and Fees*

## 101. Does the federal government pay taxes?

Agencies do pay federal taxes. They pay taxes to foreign governments if required by terms of the treaty with the foreign government. State and local taxes are another matter.

The doctrine of sovereign immunity and the Supremacy Clause of the Constitution prohibit states from taxing the federal government.[113] Although this is an easy rule to understand, applying it to the myriad complex state and local tax codes is confusing and often litigated.

Three broad categories constitute the basis for a discussion on taxes:

1. Taxes linked to business transactions involving the federal government, typically sales and use taxes
2. Federal employees incurring the payment of taxes while performing government business
3. Property-oriented taxes linked to ownership or use of various types of real and personal property.

## 102. I've heard that the federal government doesn't pay sales or use taxes. Is that true?

It depends on whom the tax is levied. If the requirement to pay a tax falls on a vendor or seller, and the seller alone is obligated to pay it, the federal government may reimburse the seller for the total cost, including the tax. On the other hand, if the tax is levied directly on the federal government as the buyer, it cannot be required to pay.[114]

In the first instance, a vendor pays sales tax to a state to purchase materials to complete a federal contract. Those taxes are part of the cost of doing business, and the government ends up paying the taxes when the vendor invoices for the work.

The second instance is illustrated by a simple Government Purchase Card transaction in a store, where the store clerk tries to add on state sales tax. Because this tax would fall directly on the federal government as the buyer, it should not be paid.

## 103. Following the same logic as with a vendor, if a federal employee pays a tax while conducting official business, then shouldn't the government reimburse the employee for the amount of the tax?

Exactly. A common example is when federal employees in travel status pay state and local hotel taxes. They are fully reimbursed for the amount of the taxes paid.

## 104. How are property taxes handled?

Federal land located within state borders is also exempt from state property taxes on the same basis that the government is immune to sales taxes.[115]

In addition, state and local entities may not levy assessments against federal land for local improvements, even if the improvements would be made to federal land. These improvements are normally for paving streets and installing sewers. Such assessments are involuntary and fit the definition of a tax.[116] However, after an analysis of the work done and the benefits provided, it may be possible to pay for such improvements on a *quantum meruit* basis.[117] A complete discussion of performing the *quantum meruit* analysis is beyond the scope of this book, and the reader is advised to read the complete exposition provided in Chapter 4 of the Redbook.

## 105. What is a possessory interest tax? I've heard it has something to do with property taxes.

Some local taxing authorities, unable to assess property taxes against federal land, have changed their property tax to a possessory interest tax. This means the tax falls on the person who has a "possessory interest" in the property. Thus, federal employees living in housing owned by the Forest Service were presented with possessory interest tax bills. Because the tax was on the federal employees, the government had to reimburse the employees for the amount of the taxes paid.[118]

## 106. Does the federal government have to pay fees levied by state and local governments?

If it truly is a fee, the government pays it. A fee means there is some value received for the services rendered and the charge is commensurate with the level of service provided. For example, the government will pay for city water consumed by the government. Toll roads charge fees, which the government pays. Tolls are considered a fee because if you don't drive on the road, you don't pay the fee.

Taxing authorities often try to call their taxes "fees." The nature of the transaction must be examined before a determination of whether to pay it can be made. Remember, agencies pay fees, but not taxes levied directly on the government.

### 107. Suppose a government employee driving a government vehicle uses a Government Purchase Card to fill the tank. The state tax on gasoline is included in the price per gallon. Clearly, the employee is not in a position to refuse to pay the state tax. How are these transactions handled?

Most gas station clerks would not take kindly to someone's refusal to pay the entire amount shown on the pump. So customers pay the entire amount, including the state tax. Then, after the fact, the government bills each state for the amount of tax it has been improperly paid. When the state sends in the money, it is considered a refund and is applied back to the appropriation account from which the original transaction took place.

## UNANSWERED PURPOSE QUESTIONS

### 108. A tremendous number of topics have been covered in this chapter on purpose. However, there are still a few topics that were not covered that I have questions on. Where do I go for the answers?

This book's aim is to answer the most frequently asked questions—those related to situations that occur in nearly every organization, again and again. Your first source of research should be Chapter 4 of the Redbook. The table of contents for Chapter 4 should reveal whether your topic is covered. If the Redbook doesn't hold your answer, go to www.gao.gov and use its search function against your key words. After that, expand your search to OMB Circulars, particularly Circular A-11. Finally, a global search of the Internet might lead you to the answer. Your agency's office of general counsel is also a valuable source of information because it has access to a broad range of legal materials and the skills needed to search them.

## NOTES

1. U.S. Government Accountability Office, *Principles of Federal Appropriations Law, Volume I* (GAO-04-261SP), Chap. 4, 4-6.
2. Ibid.
3. Ibid.
4. Ibid., 4-7.
5. Ibid.
6. Ibid., 4-9.
7. Ibid., 4-10.
8. Ibid., 4-12.
9. Ibid., 4-20.
10. Ibid.
11. Ibid., 4-21.
12. Ibid., 4-22.
13. Ibid., 4-23.
14. Ibid., 4-27.
15. Ibid., 4-28.
16. Ibid., 4-29.
17. Ibid., 4-30.
18. Ibid., 4-31.
19. Ibid.
20. Ibid.
21. Ibid., 4-33.
22. Ibid.
23. Ibid., 4-34.
24. Ibid., 4-36.
25. Ibid., 4-41.
26. Ibid., 4-37.
27. Ibid., 4-38.
28. Ibid., 4-39.
29. Ibid., 4-38.
30. Ibid., 4-44.
31. Ibid., 4-48.

32. Ibid., 4-50.
33. Ibid., 4-51.
34. Ibid., 4-100.
35. Ibid.
36. Ibid.
37. Ibid., 4-102.
38. Ibid., 4-103.
39. Ibid., 4-105.
40. Ibid., 4-106.
41. Ibid., 4-108.
42. Ibid.
43. Ibid., 4-115.
44. Ibid., 4-116.
45. Ibid., 4-120.
46. Ibid.
47. Ibid., 4-123.
48. U.S. Government Accountability Office decision, B-304718, November 9, 2005.
49. U.S. Government Accountability Office, *Principles,* Chap. 4, 4-135.
50. Ibid., 4-140.
51. U.S. Government Accountability Office decision, B-302993, June 25, 2004.
52. U.S. Government Accountability Office, *Principles,* Chap. 4, 4-132.
53. Ibid., 4-133.
54. Ibid., 4-134.
55. Ibid., 4-140.
56. Ibid., 4-142.
57. Ibid., 4-144.
58. Ibid., 4-145.
59. Ibid.
60. Ibid., 4-155.
61. Ibid., 4-156.
62. Ibid., 4-159.
63. Ibid.

64. Ibid., 4-160.
65. Ibid., 4-166.
66. Ibid., 4-169.
67. Ibid.
68. Ibid.
69. Ibid., 4-170.
70. Ibid., 4-167.
71. Ibid., 4-168.
72. Ibid., 4-176.
73. Ibid.
74. Ibid.
75. Ibid., 4-180.
76. Ibid., 4-179.
77. Ibid., 4-187.
78. Ibid., 4-234.
79. Ibid., 4-235.
80. Ibid., 4-236.
81. Ibid., 4-235.
82. Ibid., 4-234.
83. Ibid., 4-243.
84. Ibid., 4-245.
85. Ibid.
86. Ibid., 4-246.
87. Ibid., 4-250.
88. Ibid., 4-252.
89. Ibid.
90. Ibid., 4-257.
91. Ibid., 4-263.
92. Ibid., 4-262.
93. Ibid., 4-264.
94. Ibid., 4-259.
95. Ibid., 4-260.
96. Ibid., 4-265.
97. Ibid.

98. Ibid., 4-266.
99. Ibid., 4-269.
100. Ibid.
101. Ibid., 4-267.
102. Ibid., 4-268.
103. Ibid., 4-271.
104. Ibid., 4-272.
105. U.S. Government Accountability Office decision, B-307918, December 20, 2006.
106. U.S. Government Accountability Office, *Principles,* Chap. 4, 4-272.
107. Ibid., 4-274.
108. Ibid.
109. U.S. Government Accountability Office, *Principles of Federal Appropriations Law, Volume III* (GAO-08-978SP), Chap.12, 12-196.
110. Ibid., 12-197.
111. Ibid., 12-199.
112. U.S. Government Accountability Office, *Principles,* Chap. 4, 4-285.
113. Ibid., 4-286.
114. Ibid., 4-289.
115. Ibid., 4-296.
116. Ibid., 4-297.
117. Ibid., 4-298.
118. Ibid., 4-306.

# Chapter 3
# Time

As noted, there are three major elements in determining the availability and proper use of government funds— purpose, time, and amount. The previous chapter discussed purpose. This chapter is about the second element, time.

As we will see during the discussion in this chapter, Congress sets time limits for most appropriations that limit the amount of time the appropriation is available to incur new obligations. After that initial time, the appropriation remains available for adjustments and payments that liquidate the obligations.

## 109. Why does Congress put time limits on the obligation and expenditure of appropriations?

It is all part of exercising its "Power of the Purse." Congress controls executive branch spending by limiting the purpose for which funds may be spent, the amount available, and the amount of time that is available to obligate the funds, as well as setting a time limit for liquidation of the obligations. Setting time limits for obligation helps Congress to monitor execution of the appropriations and informs its resource allocation decisions in subsequent appropriations. If funds were available without any time limitations, agencies might be tempted to build up a "slush fund" over time, thereby reducing the agency's reliance on congressional appropriations.

## 110. How long are appropriations available for new obligations?

Appropriations fall into three categories, based on the duration of time in which new obligations may be created—annual, multiple-year, and no-year.[1]

Annual appropriations, also called fiscal year or one-year appropriations, are made for a specific fiscal year and are available for new obligations only during that fiscal year. The federal government's fiscal year begins October 1 and ends September 30.

All appropriations are annual appropriations unless the appropriations act specifically says otherwise. This fact is implied by the title and enacting clause of all appropriations, which says they are "for the fiscal year ending September 30, (insert calendar year)." Further, most appropriations acts include a general provision that specifically states this proposition as follows:[2]

> No part of any appropriation contained in this Act shall remain available for obligation beyond the current fiscal year unless expressly so provided herein.

Annual appropriations are available to meet only *bona fide* needs of the fiscal year for which they were enacted. The *bona fide* needs rule is discussed later in this chapter.[3]

## 111. What are multiple-year appropriations?

These are appropriations where the agency is allowed a specific amount of time—in excess of one year—to enter into obligations.[4] The nature of some commodities or transactions typically requires this extended time to execute the funds. For example, funds provided for research and development activities are usually two-year funds. Appropriations for major capital investments, such as a new computer system, are normally available for three years. Some appropriations, such as those for shipbuilding and the construction of buildings, are typically available for five years. It is up to the Congress to determine the time limits of availability.

## 112. What is a no-year appropriation?

A no-year appropriation is available for obligation without any fiscal year limitation. The appropriation must specifically indicate that it is intended to be no-year. Usually Congress uses the phrase "to remain available until expended" to create no-year appropriations; another phrase sometimes used is "without fiscal year limitation," which also suffices to make it no-year.[5]

No-year appropriations are favored by spending agencies because of the flexibility they afford. Congress is judicious in their creation because of the loss of congressional control over program levels from year to year.

### 113. What happens to funds the agency fails to obligate by the end of the appropriation's available period?

Funds that have not been obligated by the deadline are said to have "expired" and are no longer available for new obligations. Such balances remain available (generally for five additional years), however, for valid adjustments to obligations made during the period of availability.

## *BONA FIDE* NEEDS RULE

### 114. What is the *bona fide* needs rule?

First and foremost, it is important to understand that the *bona fide* needs rule is a "time" test, not a test of "necessity." The *bona fide* needs rule helps us to determine the correct fiscal year appropriation to charge for a particular transaction.

The concept goes back over 100 years to a decision that said that an appropriation should not be used to purchase an object that is not needed in the fiscal year in which it is ordered, just to fully obligate the appropriation and keep from losing the funds to expiration.[6]

Simply stated, the rule says, "Use this year's money for this year's requirements. Use next year's money for next year's requirements." Although the concept is simple, applying it to real-life situations is often complex.

Congress has enacted statutory exceptions to the *bona fide* needs rule, such as the authority to engage in multiyear contracts and the ability to cross fiscal years with one-year severable service contracts. Yet it remains an important consideration when an agency executes its budget,[7] and violating it has been the undoing of many agency personnel when doing so causes a violation of the *Antideficiency Act*.

## 115. Does the *bona fide* needs rule apply only to annual appropriations?

No. It applies to multiple-year appropriations as well. Agencies may use multiple-year appropriations for needs arising at any time during the period of availability.[8]

## 116. Suppose I have a two-year appropriation, let's say appropriated for fiscal year 2012. These funds would remain available until September 30, 2013. Do obligations that occur in FY 2013 have to satisfy needs of FY 2012, or can they be for requirements that surface in FY 2013?

FY 2012 two-year appropriations are available for requirements of either FY 2012 or FY 2013. GAO has specifically stated that "[t]here is no requirement that 2-year funds be used only for the needs of the first year of their availability."[9]

## 117. Does the *bona fide* needs rule apply to no-year appropriations?

No. With no prescribed period of availability, there is no fixed period during which the *bona fide* need must arise.[10]

## 118. Doesn't the *bona fide* needs rule make it virtually impossible to obligate expiring funds near the end of year?

Although transactions processed near the end of September are subject to additional scrutiny, and the risk of violating the *bona fide* needs rule is greater at that time, GAO has stated:

> An appropriation is just as much available to supply the needs of the [last day] of a particular year as any other day or time in the year.[11]

While end-of-the-year transactions raise the specter of the agency's "dumping" or "parking" its funds, the timing of the obligations does not, by itself, establish anything improper. Seasonal or cyclical requirements might dictate spending late in the fiscal year. Also, funds might have been reserved for contingencies or emergencies, thus delaying obligations of needed goods or services.

## *Bona Fide* Needs Rule for Materials

### 119. How is the *bona fide* needs rule applied when buying equipment or materials?

Assume you have a new workload that will begin operation December 1. You have all the required personnel and equipment to accomplish the workload except 25 desktop computers needed for data input personnel. It is now September 1, and you have enough budget authority to cover the cost of the computers. The *bona fide* needs rule precludes you from using your current-year annual funds to purchase computers that are not needed until December 1. Desktop computers are commercially available, and you can wait until October to obligate and still receive the computers in time for your December 1 startup.

On the other hand, assume the new workload begins October 2 and October 1 is a Sunday. Now you have a *bona fide* need in the current fiscal year to order the computers so you have them when you need them. Thus, procurement lead time for commercial items and for the procurement, production, and fabrication of materials not readily available shifts the *bona fide* need back into the current year. Thus, one could restate the *bona fide* needs rule to read: "When do I need to *obligate* the funds to get the item when I need it?" It becomes a matter of when the need for the obligation exists rather than when the need for the item exists.

### 120. What if you properly obligate funds for an item, and the contractor runs into some unforeseen delays that push delivery into the next fiscal year?

So long as the *bona fide* need was met when the obligation was incurred, subsequent delays do not invalidate the obligation.[12]

## 121. Stock levels in our warehouse are dangerously low because we have been using up the stock without replacement due to lack of funding. If funding becomes available late in the fiscal year, may our stock levels be replenished?

Yes. Even though the replacement stock won't be used until a subsequent fiscal year, the need exists to have sufficient stock levels in the expiring year. So you may contract in the expiring year to replenish stock levels. Such authority is not unlimited, however. GAO advises that stock levels should not exceed one year's requirements.[13]

# *Bona Fide* Needs Rule for Services

## 122. How is the *bona fide* needs rule applied to the acquisition of services?

Because of legislation passed by Congress in the 1990s, service contracts may cross fiscal years, so long as the period of performance begins in the fiscal year funding the contract. There is, however, a limitation of 12 months on severable service contracts.[14]

A severable service is one where after some level of work has been done by the contractor, the government has received the value of the work done to that point. The contract could thus be "severed" at any point, and the government would not have lost the value of the work performed to date. Examples of severable services are grass cutting, snow plowing, window washing, and equipment maintenance. The contract could be terminated at any point, and the government would have received the benefit of having its grass cut, snow plowed, windows washed, and equipment repaired. The important aspect of severable service contracts is that they may not exceed12 months.

Non-severable services are those where a deliverable is normally required at the end of the contract. Take, for example, a contract for a study with a final report. The government receives no value until the report is delivered. The rule for non-severable services is the same as that for severable—use the funds available when the contract is awarded for the entire effort, so long as the period of performance begins within that same fiscal year—but without the 12-month contract length restriction. If the study will take two years to complete, so be it.

### 123. Is training considered severable or non-severable?

Training is considered non-severable.[15] It may therefore cross fiscal years, and it is not subject to the 12-month limitation on the length of the course.

GAO has also allowed annual funds to be used for training that does not begin until the next fiscal year so long as (1) the agency can clearly demonstrate a need for the training in the current fiscal year; (2) the agency does not have control over the scheduling of the training; and (3) the time between contract award and the beginning of the training is not excessive.[16]

Here's an example: Let's say it is September 1 and you need a particular training course. You need the course as soon as possible because it's been deferred due to a lack of funding. (You'd like it to start tomorrow.) Funding becomes available, but the vendor can't schedule the training until November 15. You have satisfied all three criteria: You can demonstrate a need in the current fiscal year; you couldn't control the scheduling; and the delay between the contract and performance is not excessive. (Ninety days is probably a good rule of thumb for "excessive," although the term has not been clearly defined.)

## REPLACEMENT CONTRACTS

### 124. Suppose we award a service contract and the contractor begins work but then defaults on the contract after the new fiscal year has arrived. We still need the work finished. How do we fund the rest of the work?

When a contract is terminated for default, the original funds remain available to award a replacement contract to another contractor to complete the unfinished work.[17] This is true even if the funds have expired. Although this seems counter to the rules on the use of expired funds, think of it not as a new obligation but as a replacement obligation to cover the replacement contract.

There are restrictions on the use of replacement contracts.[18]

1. A *bona fide* need must have existed at the time of the original contract and must continue to exist up to the award of the replacement contract.
2. The replacement contract must not exceed the scope of the original contract. Changes to quantity, quality, and time are all considered out of scope and would require a new obligation citing funds available at the time the new contract is awarded.
3. The replacement contract must be awarded within a reasonable time after termination of the original contract. Excessive delays in terminating the original contract or awarding the replacement contract make it difficult to argue that a *bona fide* need continues to exist.

## 125. What if the replacement contract increases the total cost of the contract? Which year's funds are used for the cost increase?

So long as you satisfy the criteria for a replacement contract (*bona fide* need, no change in scope, no delay in award), increases in price are funded from the fiscal year of the original contract. This is nothing more than an upward adjustment of the replacement obligation that is recorded for the replacement contract.

## 126. What if there are not enough funds available in the expired account to cover the increased cost of the replacement contract?

Though it is unlikely there would be insufficient funds in the expired account, if that is the case, then don't award a replacement contract. Award a new contract, with a new obligation citing current funds for the entire amount. Replacement contracts are not mandatory; they are used at the discretion of the agency.[19]

## CONTRACT MODIFICATIONS

### 127. When a contract is modified or amended, which fiscal year is charged?

Contracts may be modified or amended for a number of reasons, and the change may be initiated by either the government or the contractor. An amendment that remains within the general scope of the contract and does not increase the price remains an obligation of the year in which the contract was executed. However, if the change causes an increase in price, then an analysis from the *bona fide* needs perspective must be performed to determine which fiscal year to charge with the modification.[20]

If the amendment is a change in scope, that is, if it exceeds the general scope of the original contract by increasing quantities, changing timelines for completion, or changing quality requirements, the modification is considered a new obligation and is charged to funds current at the time the modification is made.[21]

When the modification remains within the scope of the original contract but results in a price increase, additional analysis is required. Contracts normally contain a "Changes" clause, which provides for additional government liability due to changes in specifications, government-caused delays, changed conditions, etc. When a contract modification causes a price increase, one must determine whether the government's liability is enforceable under a provision of the original contract, such as under the "Changes" clause. If so, it is considered an "antecedent liability" and the additional costs are charged to the appropriation that was current when the original contract was executed. Because the liability existed at the time the original contract was executed, the price adjustment that takes place at a later date is considered a *bona fide* need of the same year in which the original contract was awarded.[22]

### 128. Is congressional action required to restore the expired funds to the agency so they can be used for such upward adjustments?

No. Balances in expired accounts remain available to the agency (generally for five years) without congressional action.

### 129. Are there times when the price goes up through modification and there is no change in scope, that the additional costs are not charged to the original appropriation?

If the modification is not made pursuant to a provision in the original contract, it is not an antecedent liability and funds current at the time of modification must be obligated.[23]

In addition, under cost reimbursable contracts, discretionary cost increases that exceed the funding ceiling set by the contract are charged to funds currently available at the time the discretionary increase is granted by the contracting officer.[24]

## GRANTS AND COOPERATIVE AGREEMENTS

### 130. Does the *bona fide* needs rule apply to grants and cooperative agreements?

It applies, but the *bona fide* needs analysis is very different from the analysis of contracts. The purpose of a contract is to acquire goods or services. The purpose of a grant is to provide financial assistance. Thus, the government's "need" when making grants is to make a grant to satisfy congressional intent, and the timing of the grantee's use of the funds has no bearing on assessing the agency's needs.[25]

So the *bona fide* needs analysis for grants is quite straightforward: Was the grant made during the period of availability of the appropriation used, and does it further the authorized purpose of the program legislation? If the answer is "yes," the *bona fide* needs test is satisfied.

## ADVANCE PAYMENTS

### 131. Are advance payments authorized?

Advance payments are prohibited by statute, but there are number of notable exceptions. *Advance payment* means making a payment before the work is done or goods are delivered. The purpose of the advance payment prohibition is to protect the government against nonperformance by the contractor or other supplier. Advance payments are permissible in many situations. So we have a statutory prohibition with a series of statutory and non-statutory exceptions.[26]

It is important to distinguish between the advance payment prohibition (31 U.S.C. 3324), which prohibits paying before goods and services are provided, and the *Antideficiency Act* (31 U.S.C. 1341), which prohibits payment in advance of an appropriation. It is a common mistake to confuse the two. A violation of the advance payment law might earn you an audit finding. As we will see in the next chapter, a violation of the *Antideficiency Act* can earn you the loss of employment or even some jail time.

## 132. What are some of the exceptions to the advance payment prohibition?

Major exceptions have included the following:[27]

- Salary advances to employees
- Travel and transportation advances to employees
- Tuition payments under the *Government Employees Training Act*
- Advance funding to grantees
- Gift certificates to be redeemed later at full value
- Contract financing payments authorized under the *Federal Acquisition Regulation*
- Agency head determination to be in the "public interest," with adequate security provided by the contractor
- Presidential determination to facilitate national defense
- "Fast Pay" contracts under the *Federal Acquisition Regulation*
- Publications—defined as "any publication printed, microfilmed, photocopied, or magnetically or otherwise recorded for auditory or visual usage"
- Other federal agencies
- State and local governments furnishing noncommercial services available only from the state or local government (e.g., sewer service charges, lease of state lands).

## ACCOUNT CLOSING AND CANCELLATION OF FUNDS

### 133. The period of availability (established by the appropriations act) and the expired period when new obligations are not allowed were mentioned previously. What comes after the expired period?

The so-called *Accounts Closing Law* was passed in 1990. It defines what actions are allowable during the expired period, the length of the expired period, and what happens after the expired period.

31 U.S.C. 1553(a) states:

> After the end of the period of availability for obligation of a fixed appropriation account and before the closing of that account under section 1552(a) of this title, the account shall retain its fiscal-year identity and remain available for recording, adjusting, and liquidating obligations properly chargeable to that account.[28]

31 U.S.C. 1552(a) states:

> On September 30th of the 5th year after the period of availability for obligation of a fixed appropriation account ends, the account shall be closed and any remaining balance (whether obligated or unobligated) in the account shall be canceled and thereafter shall not be available for obligation or expenditure for any purpose.[29]

Let's sort through what this means. First, the term *fixed appropriation account* means an annual or multiple-year appropriation. We'll address no-year appropriations later.

Using an FY 2012 Salaries and Expenses annual appropriation as an example, we know that the funds are available for new obligations from October 1, 2011, until September 30, 2012. During this period the agency may make new obligations, liquidate those obligations, and make upward or downward adjustments to the obligations.

The funds expire September 30, 2012, and remain expired for five years. (This is the norm. Some agencies have other periods specified by statute; for example, the Environmental Protection Agency has seven years). During this expired period the agency may liquidate valid FY 2012 obligations that were properly incurred during FY 2012 and make upward and downward adjustments to the obligations. But it may make no new obligations.

Five years later, on September 30, 2017, the account is closed and remaining funds are canceled. They are no longer available for any purpose, including obligation, adjustment, or liquidation.

## 134. What if there are still valid invoices to be paid against the closed appropriation?

The agency would make payment from any current appropriation account that is available for the same purpose. However, the cumulative total of old obligations payable from current appropriations is limited to the lesser of 1 percent of the current appropriations or the remaining balance (whether obligated or unobligated) canceled when the appropriation account is closed.[30] Thus, agencies must maintain the visibility of the appropriation balances even after they have canceled, to ensure payments do not exceed the original appropriation.

## 135. Let me see if I understand this correctly. Assume today is April 1, 2012. I have a valid unpaid invoice citing an FY 2004 appropriation that was available for three years. Those funds would have expired on September 30, 2006, and canceled on September 30, 2011, some six months ago. To pay the bill, I would have to use FY 2012 funds of the same type. Is that correct?

Almost. The original funds have canceled. However, you are allowed to use any *currently available* funds of the same type. They need not be *current year* funds. Thus, you could use any available balances from FY 2010, FY 2011, or FY 2012 because they are all still available.

## 136. Isn't the agency being hit twice for the same obligation? It had to reserve the funds in the original year, which are now lost, and then pay for it out of current funds.

That is exactly right. From a program standpoint the agency has paid twice, though only one actual payment went out the door. Agencies need to carefully review any unpaid invoices they hold to ensure such invoices are paid before the funds cancel. Paying offices should routinely make such reviews each summer and take all possible actions to pay the invoices that cite canceling funds before September 30.

## 137. Suppose an error is detected in the records of a closed account. Are we required to leave the error as is?

Agencies are required to keep accurate records. If it is determined that account balances in a closed account are wrong due to reporting or clerical errors, the agency may make corrections to its books. Such adjustments affect only the agency's records and have no effect on the availability or use of obligated or unobligated balances formerly contained in those appropriation accounts.[31]

## 138. Are there any exceptions to the accounts closing law?

One major exception to the accounts closing law, involving contractor protests, is found at 31 U.S.C. 1558(a). Such protests may be against the solicitation, proposed award, or award of a contract. The appropriation that would have funded the contract remains available for obligation for 100 days after a final ruling is made on the protest. This provision applies to protests filed with GAO, the contracting agency, a court, or the General Services Board of Contract Appeals.[32]

Another exception applies to litigation in the courts that is not part of a protest. The equity powers of the federal courts may result in decisions that delay the expiration or canceling of budget authority that had not yet terminated at the time the suit was filed. This is based on the principle that the courts are allowed to take actions to preserve the status quo of a dispute and to protect their ability to decide a case properly before them. The courts simply suspend the expiration or closing of the account by extending the term of the existing budget authority.[33]

### 139. Does sending my annual funds on an interagency order to another agency's working capital fund (which is no-year) extend the life of my appropriation?

No. The customer's funds retain their fiscal year identity until the performing agency actually does the work and earns the revenue. Agencies have even tried sending advance payments to other agencies in an attempt to keep their funds from expiring. It just doesn't work. These attempts to "park" money with another agency will be discussed in more detail in Chapter 6, Intragovernmental Transactions.

### 140. The accounts closing law addresses fixed-term (annual and multiple-year) appropriations. Does it also mention no-year appropriations?

Yes. 31 USC 1555 states that a no-year account is to be closed if (1) the agency head or the President determines that the purposes for which the appropriation was made have been fulfilled and (2) no disbursement has been made against the appropriation for two consecutive years. Both conditions must be fulfilled to close such an account. The purpose of this *United States Code* section is to allow inactive appropriations to be closed and get them off the agency's books.[34] Thus, no-year appropriations do not expire. They go directly from available to canceled.

## *BARRING ACT*

### 141. Contractors are sometimes slow to invoice for the work they do. If they wait too long to invoice, couldn't that put the agency into a position where the funds have already canceled and current funds would be required to make the payment?

That is certainly possible. Although why a contractor would want to delay submitting an invoice is unclear, it does happen from time to time, probably due to administrative error. If a valid invoice is submitted for work properly obligated, the government is required to make the payment, even if that means using current funds.

There is one exception, however: 31 U.S.C. 3702(b)(1), usually referred to as the *Barring Act*, prohibits the payment of such a claim if it has not been received within six years of the time the claim accrues. The claim would accrue when the contractor has done the work or delivered the item contracted for. The purpose of the *Barring Act* is to limit the time exposure of claims against the government, and it allows the government to dispose of its records after a reasonable amount of time. Without a time limit for the submission of claims, the government would have to keep all of its records forever.

## RATIFICATIONS

### 142. On occasion someone who is not authorized to obligate the government does it anyway. Such an unauthorized commitment may be "ratified" by a contracting officer at a later date. If the ratification occurs in a fiscal year subsequent to the original unauthorized transaction and contractor performance, which fiscal year is charged with the obligation?

When an agency examines the facts of a situation and determines that ratification is appropriate, the act of ratification turns what was an unauthorized transaction into an authorized, legal obligation. Such ratified amounts are chargeable to the fiscal year in which the need arose and the services were performed.

## NOTES

1. U.S. Government Accountability Office, *Principles of Federal Appropriations Law, Volume I* (GAO-04-261SP), Chap. 5, 5-4.
2. Ibid., 5-5.
3. Ibid., 5-6.

4. Ibid., 5-7.
5. Ibid.
6. Ibid., 5-11.
7. Ibid., 5-12.
8. Ibid., 5-14.
9. Ibid., 5-15.
10. Ibid.
11. Ibid., 5-17.
12. Ibid., 5-23.
13. Ibid.
14. Ibid., 5-25.
15. Ibid., 5-27.
16. Ibid.
17. Ibid., 5-29.
18. Ibid.
19. Ibid., 5-33.
20. Ibid.
21. Ibid.
22. Ibid., 5-35.
23. Ibid., 5-36.
24. Ibid.
25. Ibid., 5-48.
26. Ibid., 5-50.
27. Ibid., 5-51–5-66.
28. Ibid., 5-71.
29. Ibid.
30. Ibid., 5-74.
31. Ibid., 5-75.
32. Ibid., 5-89.
33. Ibid., 5-83.
34. Ibid., 5-77.

# Chapter 4
# Amount (The *Antideficiency Act*)

Having covered purpose and time in the preceding two chapters, we come to the final tenet of appropriations law—amount. It is with this aspect of fiscal law that Congress exercises its ultimate control through the *Antideficiency Act.* Although purpose and time violations are in conflict with federal law, they carry no specific penalties and are often correctable without consequences to the agency or its personnel. However, when purpose or time violations result in an "amount" violation, or the agency creates an "amount" violation on its own, the *Antideficiency Act* comes into play. Penalties for violation of the Act can be severe. It is through the possibility of sanctions under the *Antideficiency Act* that Congress can fully exercise its power of the purse.

Before discussing the *Antideficiency Act* in detail, it is first necessary to lay the groundwork for its discussion by examining the relationship between an agency's budget submission and its actual budget execution, the significance of congressional committee reports, lump sum versus line item appropriations, and how earmarks are handled.

## BUDGET SUBMISSION VERSUS BUDGET EXECUTION

### 143. Congress appropriates budget authority largely based on the budgets submitted by agencies. Must agencies execute the appropriations provided by Congress exactly as proposed in their budgets?

Any restrictions on the use of an appropriation contained in an agency budget or in congressional committee reports are not legally binding on the agency unless specified in the appropriations act itself.[1] Congress recognizes that priorities change between when a budget is submitted and when an appropriation is received and executed.

Although budgets and legislative history in committee reports are not legally binding, in practice the agency must not show complete disregard for such restrictions. The appropriations process happens annually, and an agency that shows a lack of regard for oversight or appropriations committee recommendations will likely be called to task in the next budget cycle and find its next appropriation reduced or severely limited by line item restrictions.[2]

Agencies must walk a fine line. The best advice is to first and foremost comply with the law and any executive orders. Then make sure you have complied with agency regulations. Finally, if any flexibility remains, keep the committees concerned happy.

## LUMP SUM VERSUS LINE ITEM APPROPRIATIONS AND EARMARKS

### 144. How are lump sum appropriations different from line item appropriations?

A lump sum appropriation is created to cover multiple programs, projects, activities, or items.[3] A line item appropriation is available only for the specific object described in the appropriation.[4] A form of line item appropriation is an earmark, which is simply a line item appropriation contained within a lump sum appropriation.[5]

An example of a lump sum appropriation is Salaries and Expenses, provided for "employees' salaries and all necessary expenses of the agency." Most every agency has one or more lump sum appropriations.

Less common are line item appropriations. An example would be an appropriation to construct a particular building. Another would be funding for a new financial management system.

Earmarks are the most common form of line item funding. Congress provides the agency with a lump sum appropriation but then specifies that a portion of that lump sum must be spent in a certain fashion on a particular object.

## 145. Isn't Congress trying to eliminate earmarks?

There is strong political pressure to eliminate earmarks or, as a minimum, identify their source within the Congress. This is because of the negative reputation attributed to earmarks that pundits and many in the public call "pork barrel spending"—earmarks intended to benefit a particular segment of the economy, usually within a particular congressperson's district or state.

But not all earmarks are of that nature. Many of them are simply a convenient way for Congress to make its wishes known on how it wants a particular program administered. They could just as easily be converted into stand-alone line item appropriations. These would have the same effect as an earmark without technically being an earmark.

## 146. Is there more than one kind of earmark?

There are three basic kinds, usually referred to as ceilings, floors, and fences. Let me illustrate with a hypothetical appropriation:

> For the purchase of motor vehicles, $1,000,000, provided that not to exceed $100,000 shall be used for limousines, provided that not less than $200,000 shall be used for ambulances, and further provided that $300,000 is exclusively for pickup trucks.

The first earmark, for limousines, is called a ceiling, and it uses the phrase "not to exceed" (or sometimes "not more than"). The agency may spend any amount from $0 to $100,000 on limousines, but not a penny more. Any portion of the $100,000 not spent on limousines may be used in the general appropriation for other motor vehicles.

The second earmark, for ambulances, is called a floor, indicated by the phrase "not less than." Congress inserts floors into appropriations when it fears the agency will not spend enough on a particular object that Congress believes needs more, rather than less, funding. The agency is free to spend any amount greater than $200,000, within the confines of the appropriation, on ambulances. If for some reason (say, ambulances are in short supply) the agency is unable to spend the entire $200,000 on ambulances, any amount under-executed needs to remain available as an unobligated balance within the appropriation and be allowed to expire. For example, if the agency can obligate only $150,000 on ambulances, the remaining $50,000 must not be obligated for any purpose, thus bringing the total available funding in the appropriation down to $950,000. The agency would need at least $50,000 as an unobligated balance when the appropriation expires.

The last earmark, for pickup trucks, is called a fence. It contains the aspects of both a ceiling and a floor. When Congress uses the term "exclusively for" or "shall be available only for," it wants the agency to spend exactly that amount on the particular object—no more, no less. Thus, we say that $300,000 is "fenced off" from the rest of the appropriation.

## 147. Do violations of earmarks carry the same *Antideficiency Act* implications as violations of the entire appropriation?

They do. Earmarks are considered to be appropriations in their own right. Overspending a ceiling or a fence is a violation. Underspending a floor or a fence and then obligating the money for something else is a violation.

## 148. One last question on lump sum appropriations: May an agency "zero fund" a particular program?

So long as the program is not statutorily mandatory and is not the subject of specific appropriations language, the answer is "yes." The agency must also be careful to spend the funds on some other authorized object to avoid the complications of impoundment.[6]

As previously mentioned, however, if the agency's oversight or appropriations committee has expressed an interest in a particular program's being funded, the agency, though not legally bound to support it through obligations, must be careful not to annoy the committee members.

## *ANTIDEFICIENCY ACT*

### 149. The *Antideficiency Act* has been mentioned several times in preceding chapters. Can you summarize the basic requirements of the *Antideficiency Act*?

GAO issued a decision in 1962 (42 Comp. Gen. 272, 275) that summarizes the requirements in one paragraph:

> These statutes evidence a plain intent on the part of the Congress to prohibit executive officers, unless otherwise authorized by law, from making contracts involving the Government in obligations for expenditures or liabilities beyond those contemplated and authorized for the period of availability of and within the amount of the appropriation under which they are made; to keep all the departments of the Government, in the matter of incurring obligations for expenditures, within the limits and purposes of appropriations annually provided for conducting their lawful function, and to prohibit any officer or employee of the Government from involving the Government in any contract or other obligation for the payment of money for any purpose, in advance of appropriations made for such purpose; and to restrict the use of annual appropriation to expenditures required for the service of the particular fiscal year for which they are made.[7]

This summary has often been quoted in subsequent *Antideficiency Act* cases.

### 150. Can you break the *Antideficiency Act* down into its individual elements?

GAO has broken it down as follows:[8]

> The law prohibits:
>
> - Making or authorizing an expenditure from, or creating or authorizing an obligation under, any appropriation or fund in

excess of the amount available in the appropriation or fund unless authorized by law (31 U.S.C. 1341(a)(1)(A)).

- Involving the government in any contract or other obligation for the payment of money for any purpose in advance of appropriations made for such purpose, unless the contract or obligation is authorized by law (31 U.S.C. 1341(a)(1)(B)).
- Accepting voluntary services for the United States, or employing personal services in excess of that authorized by law, except in cases of emergency involving the safety of human life or the protection of property (31 U.S.C. 1342).
- Making obligations or expenditures in excess of an apportionment or reapportionment, or in excess of the amount permitted by agency regulations (31 U.S.C. 1517(a)).

Bear in mind that the basic principles are really quite simple: Government officials may not make payments or commit the United States to make payments at some future time for goods or services unless there is enough money in the appropriation or apportionment to cover the cost in full.

## 151. Don't violations of the purpose law and the *bona fide* needs rule constitute violations of the *Antideficiency Act*?

Violations of the purpose law (31 U.S.C. 1301) and time restrictions, including the *bona fide* needs rule (31 U.S.C. 1502), might result in violations of the *Antideficiency Act*—or they might not. The *Antideficiency Act* is violated only when the amount in an appropriation or other subdivision of funds is breached. Although many *Antideficiency Act* violations are caused by purpose violations or time violations, not all purpose and time violations create *Antideficiency Act* violations. The relationship between purpose and time violations and the *Antideficiency Act* will be discussed in more detail later.

## 152. What is the key provision of the *Antideficiency Act*?

The central provision of the *Antideficiency Act* is 31 U.S.C. 1341(a)(1), which states:

> (a)(1) An officer or employee of the United States Government or of the District of Columbia government may not—
>
> (A) make or authorize an expenditure or obligation exceeding an amount available in an appropriation or fund for the expenditure or obligation; or
>
> (B) involve either government in a contract or obligation for the payment of money before an appropriation is made unless authorized by law.

In the beginning, this was the only provision of the *Antideficiency Act*. Congress subsequently added other provisions to ensure compliance with this basic prohibition.[9]

## 153. Am I to understand that the *Antideficiency Act* can be violated at the time of obligation, not just when the payment becomes due?

That is correct. The act of obligating the United States to make a payment is a violation if sufficient budget authority is not already in the agency's account.[10]

## 154. Section 1341 states that a violation occurs when funds are obligated or spent in excess or advance of an "appropriation or fund." Can you describe what is meant by "appropriation or fund"?

The phrase refers to appropriation and fund accounts held by the Treasury. An *appropriation account* is the basic unit of an appropriation that reflects each unnumbered paragraph of an appropriations act. Fund accounts include general fund accounts, intragovernmental fund accounts, special fund accounts, and trust fund accounts. Revolving funds, such as working capital funds, are likewise prohibited from overobligating available budget authority or overdisbursing their fund balances with the Treasury.[11]

Not every transaction using federal funds constitutes an obligation or expenditure, however. For example, section 1341 applies to Indian trust funds managed by the Bureau of Indian Affairs. But when the Bureau invested some of those funds in certificates of deposit with federally insured banks (which was authorized by statute), GAO determined that investing is not obligating or expending. Thus, even the act of overinvesting such trust funds does not violate the *Antideficiency Act* unless or until such overinvested funds are actually obligated or expended by the Bureau.[12]

## 155. Is year-end the only time I need to worry about *Antideficiency Act* violations? How about end-of-quarter or end-of-month?

An *Antideficiency Act* violation can occur at any time, not just at the end of a fiscal period. Although the end of a year or quarter is when an agency is most vulnerable, because of the lapsing of appropriation or apportionment balances, care must be taken to avoid an overobligation at any moment in time.

## 156. If the obligations recorded in my accounting system exceed my appropriation, have I automatically violated the *Antideficiency Act*?

Section 1501 of Title 31 requires agencies to promptly and properly record all obligations. Therefore, recorded obligations in excess of the available appropriation are *prima facie* evidence of a violation of the *Antideficiency Act*. However, this is not conclusive evidence that a violation has occurred.[13] Agencies often make mistakes. They sometimes record as obligations transactions that are not truly obligations. They might overstate the amount of the true obligation when recording it. They might record transactions as obligations before the obligation actually exists. In all of these situations, if review and adjustment of the accounting records shows that the level of actual obligations never exceeded the available appropriation, then no violation has occurred.

On the other hand, agencies often make mistakes in the opposite direction when recording obligations. They sometimes fail to record an obligation or do not record it in a timely manner. They also might under-record the amount of the obligation. Or they might record it to the wrong account. In these instances, although the accounting records might show an available balance, when the obligations are eventually posted correctly, they might reveal that a violation has occurred. Failing to record an obligation or improperly posting one does not relieve the agency's responsibility to report all actual violations.[14]

The point here is that an obligation or expenditure posted in the accounting records merely evidences the obligation or disbursement; it doesn't create it. Funds are obligated or expended by authorized officials, such as contracting officers and disbursing officers. They exist regardless of whether they are posted as such in the agency's books.

Therefore, whenever a violation is suspected, a thorough understanding of what constitutes an obligation, and when it occurs, is necessary. Agency officials must be familiar with the provisions of 31 U.S.C. 1501. Chapter 7 of the *Principles of Federal Appropriations Law* should also be consulted for guidance.

## *Indemnification Agreements*

### 157. What is an indemnification agreement?

Under an *indemnification agreement*, one party to the agreement—the government, for *Antideficiency Act* purposes—promises to cover another party's losses. The federal government has very deep pockets, so it is not surprising that contractors and state or local governments frequently ask that their risk of loss be covered.[15]

### 158. An indemnification agreement somehow seems like an extension of the federal government's policy of self-insurance. What is wrong with the government's also insuring against contractors' or other government entities' losses when they are doing work for the federal government?

The problem is that if the amount of the government's liability is indefinite, indeterminate, or potentially unlimited, the *Antideficiency Act* will be violated because appropriations are finite sums. The potential liability is greater than any appropriation ever passed. Therefore, both GAO and the courts have consistently ruled that without specific statutory authority the government may not enter into such an unlimited agreement and that doing so automatically constitutes a violation of the *Antideficiency Act*.[16]

## *Purpose and Time Violations versus Antideficiency Act*

### 159. What is the relationship between the purpose law and the *Antideficiency Act*?

This section will cover how to determine when and to what extent a purpose violation also violates the *Antideficiency Act*. 63 Comp. Gen. 422, 424 (1984) offers a useful starting point for this discussion:

> Not every violation of 31 USC 1301(a) also constitutes a violation of the Antideficiency Act.... Even though an expenditure may have been charged to an improper source, the Antideficiency Act's prohibition against incurring obligations in excess or in advance of available appropriations is not also violated unless no other funds were available for that expenditure. Where, however, no other funds were authorized to be used for the purpose in question (or where those authorized were already obligated), both 31 USC 1301(a) and 1341(a) have been violated. In addition, we would consider an Antideficiency Act violation to have occurred where an expenditure was improperly charged and the appropriate fund source, although available at the time, was subsequently obligated, making readjustment of accounts impossible.[17]

### 160. Why does it matter whether an agency breaks one law or two laws?

It matters because *Antideficiency Act* violations carry statutory reporting requirements and potentially severe penalties. Purpose law violations often arise from simple mistakes in posting obligations and are easily fixed by reversing the problem transaction—so long as the *Antideficiency Act* has not also been violated at the same time.

## 161. Can you summarize that Comptroller General decision (63 Comp. Gen. 422, 424 (1984) regarding the applicability of the *Antideficiency Act*?

The gist of it is that a purpose law violation doesn't automatically violate the *Antideficiency Act*, so long as it can be determined, once the correct appropriation is charged and the purpose law violation fixed, that sufficient proper budget authority was available at the time of the obligation and was continuously available ever since. In other words, if the original mistake of charging the wrong appropriation had not been made, and the correct appropriation had been charged, would the *Antideficiency Act* have been violated? If the answer is "no," because there would have been no question about funding availability if the correct appropriation had been charged, then no *Antideficiency Act* violation exists.

Another way to look at it is that the *Antideficiency Act* applies to only the *amount* available for obligation or disbursement. Purpose law violations (and time or *bona fide* needs violations) often lead to *Antideficiency Act* violations but do not by themselves constitute *Antideficiency Act* violations.

## 162. Can you provide some examples of purpose and time violations and how it is determined that an *Antideficiency Act* violation has occurred?

Suppose an agency charges an obligation or disbursement to the wrong appropriation account, either charging the wrong appropriation for the correct time period or charging the wrong fiscal year. If the appropriation that should have been charged in the first place had sufficient funds and has continued to have sufficient funds, allowing for adjustment of the accounts, no *Antideficiency Act* violation has occurred.

A 1994 decision (73 Comp. Gen. 259) documents a case in which an agency erroneously charged some furniture to the wrong appropriation but had sufficient funds in the proper account to support an adjustment correcting the error. GAO concluded that no *Antideficiency Act* violation had occurred.

On the other hand, a violation exists if the proper account does not have enough money to permit the adjustment, including cases in which sufficient funds were available at the time of the error but were not continuously available until the time of correction. This finding is supported by 70 Comp. Gen. 592 (1991) and B-222048, February 10, 1987.[18]

Other relevant cases involved grant funds charged to the wrong fiscal year, contract modifications charged to expired accounts rather than to current appropriations, and items that should have been charged to other operating appropriations charged instead to the General Services Administration working capital fund.[19]

## 163. If Congress specifically prohibits the purchase of a certain commodity, could such a purchase trigger a violation?

Absolutely. Prohibitions come from several sources. Sometimes authorization acts or other general statutes contain language forbidding the purchase of certain items or services.

The Employment Standards Administration (ESA), Department of Labor, reported a violation in FY 2007 that illustrates this concept. Federal law prohibits federal agencies from paying an employee who is not a citizen of the United States and does not meet certain exceptions. ESA paid over $29,000 to an employee who was a Mexican citizen. This violated 31 U.S.C. 1341 because the amount available for payment to non-U.S. citizens is zero.[20]

GAO decisions are another source of prohibitions against the purchase of particular commodities. Examples include gifts to employees, reimbursement for commuting to work in a privately owned vehicle, and greeting cards.

Finally, appropriations acts typically contain many prohibitions. These usually contain language such as "None of the funds provided under this or any other act shall be used for . . . ." The FY 2008 *Consolidated*

*Appropriations Act* contains a host of prohibitions against paying for particular commodities, including:[21]

- Construction or repair of National Oceanic and Atmospheric Administration (NOAA) vessels in foreign shipyards
- Promoting the sale or export of tobacco products
- Issuing patents encompassing a human organism
- Supporting the use of torture by any United States government official or contract employee
- Purchasing first class or premium airline travel in contravention of Title 41 of the *Code of Federal Regulations*
- Sending more than 50 employees from a federal department or agency to, or paying for their attendance at, any single conference occurring outside the United States.

In all of these situations, obligating or disbursing federal funds for prohibited or unauthorized goods or services constitutes a violation of the *Antideficiency Act*. The Comptroller General stated this principle very clearly in a 1981 decision:

> When an appropriations act specifies that an agency's appropriation is not available for a designated purpose, and the agency has no other funds available for that purpose, any officer of the agency who authorizes an obligation or expenditure of agency funds for that purpose violates the *Antideficiency Act*. Since the Congress has not appropriated funds for the designated purpose, the obligation may be viewed either as being in excess of the amount (zero) available for that purpose or as in advance of appropriations made for that purpose. In either case the *Antideficiency Act* is violated.[22]

Examples of violations where agencies ignored a statutory restriction abound:[23]

- Use of funds in violation of a statutory prohibition against publicity or propaganda
- Appropriations used for unauthorized technical assistance

- Violation of an appropriation rider prohibiting the use of funds to implement an OMB memorandum
- Appropriation used to procure unauthorized legal services
- Unauthorized use of a Training and Employment Services Account appropriation
- Violation of a "Buy American" provision in an appropriations act
- Reprogramming of funds for an unauthorized purpose
- An employee detail (temporary work assignment) that is contrary to a specific statutory prohibition.

### 164. When an illegal contracting document is issued (for example, for bottled water) and payment is subsequently made, who is named in the *Antideficiency Act* violation report—the funds-authorizing and contracting officials or the certifying officer?

It is up to the agency to determine who the culprits are. Although the acts of certifying and disbursing created the *Antideficiency Act* violation, most agencies will cite the funds-authorizing official on the front end of the transaction as the person who caused the violation. Had the funds-authorizing official not approved the use of the funds for the item, the certifying officer would not have been put into the position of certifying the transaction for payment.

Further, funds-authorizing officials tend to be of a higher grade than certifying officers and are thus expected to "know better." In addition, the certifying officers have pecuniary liability to worry about, which is not a concern of the funds-authorizing official.

## *Exceptions*

### 165. Are there any exceptions to the *Antideficiency Act*?

There are several, all based in law. The Act itself recognizes that Congress may grant exceptions. Section 1341 of Title 31 prohibits obligations or expenditures in advance or excess of available appropriations "unless authorized by law." This is a clear recognition that Congress may authorize exceptions to the laws it passes.[24]

## 166. Can you provide some examples of exceptions to the *Antideficiency Act*?

A major category of exceptions is broadly described as *contract authority*, which is defined as the statutory authority to enter into binding contracts without the funds adequate to make payments under them.[25] Contract authority is one of several types of budget authority described in OMB Circular A-11.

The term *contract authority* as used in this context must not be confused with the "authority to enter into contracts." An agency does not need specific authority to enter into contracts. This legal authority to enter into contracts does not constitute an exception to the *Antideficiency Act*. To constitute an exception to the Act, a contract authorized by law requires the authority to enter into such contract without regard to the availability of appropriations. This authority must be provided to an agency by statute.

## 167. What is the value of a contract that an agency can't make payments against?

Contract authority is extremely valuable in certain situations. A common use is to finance the purchase of inventory through a revolving fund. The idea is that contract authority allows the revolving fund to contract for large amounts of inventory without tying up its fund balance. The inventory purchased may have long manufacturing times, sometimes years. Rather than encumber very limited revolving fund balances for an extended period, contract authority is granted by Congress to enter into contracts for such inventory. Ultimately, the liquidations of the obligations incurred are financed by the revolving fund through the sale of the inventory to the revolving fund customers.

## 168. Is contract authority ever provided to agencies funded by direct appropriations, and if so, doesn't that limit Congress' future flexibility to decide how to appropriate funds?

Congress provides contract authority to direct-funded agencies on occasion. Contract authority does necessitate a commitment on Congress' part to follow through with a liquidating appropriation at a later date.

# *Apportionment*

## 169. What is apportionment?

*Apportionment* is a process by which, as the name suggests, appropriated funds are distributed to agencies in portions over the period of availability. OMB apportions funds for executive branch agencies. Appropriations for the legislative branch, the judiciary, the District of Columbia, and the International Trade Commission are apportioned by officials having administrative control of those funds.[26] The term *apportionment* is officially defined as follows:

> The action by which [the apportioning official] distributes amounts available for obligation, including budgetary reserves established pursuant to law, in an appropriation or fund account. An apportionment divides amounts available for obligation by specific time periods (usually quarters), activities, projects, objects, or a combination thereof. The amounts so apportioned limit the amount of obligations that may be incurred. An apportionment may be further subdivided by an agency into allotments, suballotments, and allocations. In apportioning any account, some funds may be reserved to provide for contingencies or to effect savings made possible pursuant to the *Antideficiency Act*. Funds apportioned to establish a reserve must be proposed for deferral or recission pursuant to the *Impoundment Control Act of 1974* (2 U.S.C. 681–688).
>
> The apportionment process is intended to (1) prevent the obligation of amounts available within an appropriation or fund

account in a manner that would require deficiency or supplemental appropriations and (2) achieve the most effective and economical use of amounts made available for obligation.[27]

## 170. Is an obligation or expenditure in advance of or in excess of an apportionment a violation of the *Antideficiency Act*?

Yes. Section 1517(a)(1) of Title 31 prohibits such obligations or expenditures. GAO stated in B290600, July 10, 2002:

> The Antideficiency Act prohibits . . . the making or the authorizing of obligations or expenditures in advance of, or in excess of, available appropriations. . . . An agency may obligate an appropriation only after OMB has apportioned it to the agency.

## 171. Is obligating or expending funds in excess of an allotment, suballotment, allocation, or other administrative subdivision of funds an *Antideficiency Act* violation?

OMB Circular A-11 is the controlling regulation for allotments and suballotments. It states that overobligation or overexpenditure of allotments or suballotments is ***always*** a violation.

Overobligation or overexpenditure of other administrative subdivisions is a violation only if an agency's fund control regulations define them as such.[28] OMB's guidance is consistent with the language found in 31 U.S.C. 1517(a)(2) and 1514(a).

### *Voluntary Services*

## 172. What does the Voluntary Services section of the *Antideficiency Act* say?

Section 1342 of Title 31 reads:

> An officer or employee of the United States Government or of the District of Columbia government may not accept

voluntary services for either government or employ personal services exceeding that authorized by law except for emergencies involving the safety of human life or the protection of property . . . .

## 173. Does the Voluntary Services prohibition tie in with the prohibition against augmentation?

Indeed it does. An objective of the *Antideficiency Act* was to keep an agency's level of operations within the amounts Congress appropriates for that purpose. The use of voluntary services would permit circumvention of that objective because such a practice augments an appropriation.[29] Funds not paid for such voluntary services are then available for other purposes. Receiving voluntary services is tantamount to receiving additional budget authority. Congress jealously guards its power of the purse and prohibits such external funding sources.

## 174. Are agencies also prohibited from accepting voluntary services from sources other than government employees?

The general answer is "yes." Agencies should not accept the services of outsiders to accomplish tasks that should be done by government employees.[30] Accepting outside services is another example of augmentation of an appropriation. However, a 1913 attorney general opinion made a distinction between voluntary services and gratuitous services. Only voluntary services are prohibited.

## 175. What is the difference between voluntary services and gratuitous services?

A 1913 attorney general opinion addressed whether a retired army officer could be employed as superintendent of an Indian school without additional compensation. The attorney general replied that the appointment would not violate the voluntary services prohibition of section 1342. The attorney general's opinion discusses the distinction between the two terms:

> [I]t seems plain that the words "voluntary service" were not intended to be synonymous with "gratuitous service" and were not intended to cover services rendered in an official capacity under regular appointment to an office otherwise permitted by law to be non-salaried. In their ordinary and normal meaning these words refer to service intruded by a private person as a "volunteer" and not rendered pursuant to any prior contract or obligation. . . . It would be stretching the language a good deal to extend it so far as to prohibit *official* services without compensation in those instances in which Congress has not required even a minimum salary for the office.
>
> The context corroborates the view that the ordinary meaning of "voluntary services" was intended. The very next words "or employ personal services in excess of that authorized by law" deal with *contractual* services, thus making a balance between "acceptance" of "voluntary service" (*i.e.*, the cases where there is no prior contract) and "employment" of "personal service" (*i.e.*, the cases where there is such prior contract, though unauthorized by law).
>
> Thus it is evident that the evil at which Congress was aiming was not appointment or employment for authorized services without compensation, but the acceptance of unauthorized services not intended or agreed to be gratuitous and therefore likely to afford a basis for a future claim upon Congress. . . .[31]

The comptroller of the Treasury agreed with the attorney general's interpretation. The comptroller, and subsequently GAO and the Justice Department, adopted this position and continue to follow it. The comptroller wrote:

> [The statute] was intended to guard against claims for compensation. A service offered clearly and distinctly as gratuitous with a proper record made of that fact does not violate this statute against acceptance of voluntary service. An appointment to serve without compensation which is accepted and properly recorded is not a violation of [31 USC 1342], and is valid if otherwise lawful.[32]

Two main rules govern voluntary and gratuitous services. First, if compensation for a position is fixed by law, an appointee may not agree to serve without compensation or to waive that compensation in whole or in part. Actually, this portion of the opinion was not really new. The courts had already held that compensation fixed by law could not be waived. Second, if the level of compensation is discretionary, or if the relevant statute prescribes only a maximum but not a minimum, the compensation may be set at zero, and an appointment without compensation or a waiver, entire or partial, is permissible.[33]

## 176. Don't some agencies routinely violate 31 U.S.C. 1342 by allowing employees to work extra hours without providing overtime pay or compensatory time off?

Most likely. Employees who are covered by the *Fair Labor Standards Act* (FLSA)—non-exempt employees—are entitled to payment for extra hours worked, or they may agree to accept compensatory time in lieu of payment. Federal managers must be very careful not to direct such employees to work overtime without compensation. They must be equally careful not to "suffer or permit" to work overtime eager non-exempt employees who are just trying to do a good job. The law is clear: Accepting such voluntary services constitutes a violation of the *Antideficiency Act.*

## 177. Has anyone ever actually reported a violation of 31 U.S.C. 1342?

Such a case was reported in 2005. U.S. Army National Guard civilians had worked on a weekend, without compensation, to deliver training to National Guard members.[34]

# THE PROHIBITION OF AUGMENTATION

## 178. What is the rationale for the rule against augmentation of an agency's appropriations?

The objective of the rule against augmentation of appropriations is to prevent an agency from undercutting congressional power by circuitously exceeding the amount Congress has appropriated for that activity. A recent decision (B-300248, January 15, 2004) put it this way:

> When Congress establishes a new program or activity, it also must decide how to finance it. Typically it does this by appropriating funds from the U.S. Treasury. In addition to providing necessary funds, a congressional appropriation establishes a maximum authorized program level, meaning that an agency cannot, absent statutory authorization, operate beyond the level that can be paid for by its appropriations. An agency may not circumvent these limitations by augmenting its appropriations from sources outside the government. One of the objectives of these limitations is to prevent agencies from avoiding or usurping Congress' "power of the purse."[35]

## 179. Is there a specific statute forbidding augmentation?

There is no single statute that explicitly prohibits the augmentation of appropriated funds. The concept can be derived from several separate enactments:[36]

- 31 U.S.C. 3302(b), the miscellaneous receipts statute.
- 31 U.S.C. 1301(a), the purpose law, which restricts the use of appropriated funds to their intended purposes. Early comptroller of the Treasury decisions often used 31 U.S.C. 3302(b) and 1301(a) as a basis of support for prohibiting augmentation.
- 18 U.S.C. 209, which prohibits the payment of, contribution to, or supplementation of the salary of a government officer or employee as compensation for his or her official duties by any source other than the government of the United States.

## 180. How are augmentation and the *Antideficiency Act* related?

If an agency augments its appropriation without statutory authority, and then obligates those augmented amounts, the agency would exceed its appropriated level. Hence, this action would constitute a violation of the *Antideficiency Act*.

One common example is the prohibition against transfers between appropriations without specific statutory authority. An unauthorized transfer is an improper augmentation of the receiving appropriation.[37] Note that the transfer prohibition and the augmentation rule do not apply to reprogramming actions at the agency allotment level within the same appropriation. In these situations, the total amount available in a given appropriation remains constant. Transfers between appropriations, on the other hand, decrease the size of one appropriation and increase the size of another.

There is a rule that a general appropriation may not be used if a more specific appropriation for an object is available. If a specific appropriation is exhausted, agencies may be tempted to use a more general appropriation to continue operations. However, such a practice violates 31 U.S.C. 1301(a), using a general appropriation for an unauthorized purpose, and also improperly augments the specific appropriation.

Although the augmentation rule is related to the concept of purpose availability, it is most closely related to the availability of an amount of funds because it restricts executive spending to the amounts appropriated by Congress. In this respect, it is a logical and indispensable complement to the *Antideficiency Act*.[38]

## *Miscellaneous Receipts*

### 181. What is the miscellaneous receipts statute?

The miscellaneous receipts statute is found at 31 U.S.C. 3302(b). It was enacted in 1849 and states:

> Except as provided in section 3718(b) of this title, an official or agent of the Government receiving money for the Government from any source shall deposit the money in the Treasury as soon as practicable without deduction for any charge or claim.

Penalties for violation are found in 31 U.S.C. 3302(d). They allow for the violator to be removed from office and required to forfeit any money held, including such funds to which the violator might otherwise be entitled.[39]

## 182. What does the miscellaneous receipts statute mean in practice?

Any money an agency receives on behalf of the government from a source outside the agency must be deposited in the Treasury. This means that the money must be deposited into the general fund ("miscellaneous receipts") of the Treasury, ***not*** into the agency's own appropriation. The comptroller of the Treasury explained the distinction between the two in 22 Comp. Dec. 379, 381 (1916):

> It [31 USC 3302(b)] could hardly be made more comprehensive as to the moneys that are meant and these moneys are required to be paid "into the Treasury." This does not mean that the moneys are to be added to a fund that has been appropriated *from* the Treasury and may be in the Treasury or outside. It seems to me that it can only mean that they shall go into the general fund of the Treasury which is subject to any disposition which Congress might choose to make of it. This has been the holding of the accounting officers for many years. If Congress intended that these moneys should be returned to the appropriation from which a similar amount had once been expended it could have been readily so stated, and it was not.[40]

## 183. Once an agency deposits money received into a miscellaneous receipts account, is it then barred from taking the funds back out?

Yes. That is exactly why the miscellaneous receipts statute is so significant in ensuring that the executive branch remains dependent upon the congressional appropriation process. Recall the provision in article I, section 9, clause 7, of the U.S. Constitution: "No money shall be drawn from the Treasury but in consequence of appropriations made by law." Once money is deposited into a miscellaneous receipts account, it takes an appropriation to get it out.[41]

## 184. Am I correct in assuming that depositing a miscellaneous receipt into an agency's appropriation, rather than depositing it with Treasury, would constitute an augmentation of the appropriation?

Yes. Such an action would constitute an improper augmentation of the appropriation to which the money was deposited.

## 185. No-year appropriations seem to have much more flexibility than fixed-term appropriations. Does the miscellaneous receipts statute apply to these funds as well?

The statute applies even for no-year appropriations. The no-year status relates to the duration of availability of the funds, not to the amount.[42]

## 186. Are there any exceptions to the miscellaneous receipts statute?

Exceptions fall into two broad categories, statutory and nonstatutory.[43]

- An agency may retain money it receives if it has statutory authority to do so. In other words, 31 U.S.C. 3302(b) will not apply if there is specific statutory authority for the agency to retain the funds.
- Receipts that qualify as repayments to an appropriation may be retained to the credit of that appropriation and are not required to be deposited into the general fund of the Treasury. These repayments may be further divided into two general classes, reimbursements and refunds.[44]
  - *Reimbursements* are sums received as a result of commodities sold or services furnished either to the public or to another government account, which are authorized by law to be credited directly to a specific appropriation.
  - *Refunds* are repayments for excess payments and are to be credited to the appropriation or fund accounts from which the excess payments were made. They must be directly related to previously recorded expenditures and are reductions of those expenditures.

Refunds to appropriations represent amounts collected from outside sources for payments made in error, overpayments, or adjustments for previous amounts disbursed. Refunds constitute the non-statutory exception to the miscellaneous receipts statute. The rationale for this exception is to enable an appropriation account to be made whole by retaining a refund that was the result of an overpayment. GAO decision B-302366, July 12, 2004, states that crediting a refund to an appropriation "simply restores to the appropriation amounts that should not have been paid from the appropriation."

## 187. What are the specific statutory exceptions to the miscellaneous receipts statute?

They are too numerous to list. Title 10 of the *United States Code* spells out several exceptions for DoD, including proceeds from agricultural and grazing leases, sale or lease of real property, hunting and fishing permits, and recycling programs.

Non-DoD examples include 42 U.S.C. 8287 and 8256, which allow retention of savings from energy savings performance contracts and rebates from utility companies for energy-saving measures.[45]

A major exception that applies to every federal agency is the *Economy Act*, 31 U.S.C. 1535 and 1536, which is discussed in more detail later in this chapter. *The Economy Act* allows agencies to collect reimbursement for work performed on behalf of another agency into their own appropriations. Without the Act, intragovernmental reimbursable work would not be possible; any money collected from a customer would have to be deposited into miscellaneous receipts.

### *Loss of or Damage to Government Property*

## 188. May an agency retain money it recovers for loss of or damage to government property to pay for replacement or repair?

The general answer is "no," but there are exceptions. Normally, funds recovered for the loss of or damage to government property must be deposited in the Treasury as miscellaneous receipts. The rationale is that appropriations provide agencies with funding to repair or replace damaged or lost property, regardless of how it was damaged or lost.

There are statutory exceptions to this general rule. For example, 40 U.S.C. 321 provides that GSA may credit recoveries for loss or damage to General Supply Fund property to the General Supply Fund. Likewise, under 16 U.S.C. 579c, the U.S. Forest Service is authorized to retain money received from a settlement for damage to land—for example, pursuant to a timber sale.[46]

Additionally, a recent GAO decision determined that damages recovered by revolving funds may be retained by the revolving fund and are not subject to the miscellaneous receipts statute. The idea behind this decision is that such loss or damage is a cost of doing business, and recoveries should make the fund whole for the losses incurred. However, any amount recovered that is beyond the cost of actual loss or damage must be deposited with Treasury as a miscellaneous receipt.[47]

## 189. May the person who lost or damaged government property simply replace it or have it repaired from his or her own funds?

GAO has consistently allowed this practice as a non-statutory exception, even though it seems as if the agency would be doing something indirectly that it may not do directly, thereby bypassing the statute.

It is permissible for a private party responsible for loss or damage to government property to agree to replace it in kind or have it repaired to the satisfaction of the agency and to make payment directly to the party making the repairs. The agency is not required to transfer an amount equal to the cost of the repair or replacement to miscellaneous receipts. This principle was first recognized in 14 Comp. Dec. 310 (1907), and it has been followed ever since. The exception applies even though the money would have to go to miscellaneous receipts if the responsible party had paid it directly to the government.[48]

## 190. Suppose one federal agency damages the property of another federal agency. Must the first agency pay for the damage, and may the agency that owns the property retain such payment?

The general rule under the interdepartmental waiver doctrine is that funds available to the agency that causes the damage may not be used to pay claims for damages by the agency whose property was damaged. This doctrine is based on the concept that agencies' property is the property not of separate entities but rather of the government as a single entity, and there can be no reimbursement by the government for damages to or loss of its own property. Thus, under this rule, one agency may not make payment to another federal agency for damages it caused.[49]

However, there is a well-established exception to this rule. In B-302962, June 10, 2005, GAO explained it:

> The interdepartmental waiver doctrine does not apply . . . where an agency has statutory authority to retain income derived from the use or sale of certain property, and the governing legislation shows an intent for the particular program or activity to be self-sustaining. 24 Comp. Gen. 847 (1945). Thus, where an agency operation is financed through reimbursement or a revolving fund, the prohibition does not apply. 65 Comp. Gen. 910 (1986). In such cases, the agency should recover amounts sufficient to cover loss or damage to property financed by the reimbursements or revolving fund, regardless of whether that damage is caused by another federal agency or a private party, and deposit those funds into the revolving fund. The rationale for this exception is that the revolving fund, established to operate like a self-sustaining business, should not bear the cost for "other than objects for which the fund was created."[50]

Thus, funds recovered from another federal agency for damage to revolving-fund property may be retained by the revolving fund and are not subject to the miscellaneous receipts statute.

## Fees, Fines, and Penalties

### 191. Federal agencies sometimes collect fees, which are designed to offset the cost of providing a service. An example is fees collected under the *Freedom of Information Act*. Are such fees credited to agency appropriations or to the Treasury as miscellaneous receipts?

Numerous GAO decisions all boil down to one basic rule: If an agency is to retain the fees collected in its appropriation and use them, the agency must have (1) statutory authority to charge fees for its programs and activities *and* (2) statutory authority to retain and use the fees collected.[51]

For example, collection of *Freedom of Information Act* fees is authorized, but they must be deposited as miscellaneous receipts. The rationale is that the government should be compensated for the significant costs associated with researching and copying documents in response to a FOIA request, but the agency is funded by appropriations to comply with FOIA requirements. Therefore, agencies may collect the fees but not retain them.[52]

### 192. How are fines and penalties received by the government handled?

Absent statutory authority to retain them, monies collected as a fine or penalty must be deposited in the Treasury as miscellaneous receipts under 31 U.S.C. 3302(b).[53] The rule for fees also applies to fines and penalties. The agency must have the statutory authority to impose and collect a fine or penalty, as well as the statutory authority to retain such fines and penalties. Without both, fines and penalties go to the Treasury.

## *ECONOMY ACT* REIMBURSEMENTS AND REVOLVING FUNDS

### 193. Does the *Economy Act*, which authorizes an agency to retain reimbursement for work performed on behalf of another agency, constitute a statutory exception to the miscellaneous receipts statute?

Indeed it does. In fact, were it not for the *Economy Act* and similar subsequent pieces of specific legislation, the concept of reimbursement within the federal government would not exist.

The *Economy Act*, 31 U.S.C. 1535 and 1536, authorizes the inter- and intradepartmental furnishing of materials or performance of work or services on a reimbursable basis. This statutory exception to the miscellaneous receipts statute authorizes a performing agency to credit reimbursements to the appropriation or fund charged in executing its performance.[54]

### 194. What sort of costs may the performing agency recoup for *Economy Act* work?

Although the allowable costs are normally agreed to in advance by the performing agency and the ordering agency, certain guidelines should be followed.

Agencies should "get what they pay for, and pay for what they get." In other words, a reimbursement must be for actual costs incurred. If the performing agency charges more than its actual costs, its appropriation would be augmented. If it charges less than the actual costs, the ordering agency's appropriation would be augmented. Thus, although there is some flexibility in determining costs, they must be reasonable to avoid an augmentation. Generally speaking, an agency should charge for only the incremental, or out-of-pocket, costs associated with fulfilling the agreement. General and administrative or other fixed costs should not be included.

Also, reimbursement may not be credited to an appropriation against which no charges have been made in executing the order because that would constitute an improper augmentation. An example would be crediting reimbursement for depreciation to an appropriation that did not bear any costs of the transaction. If a specific procurement appropriation had been used to purchase a piece of equipment, it would be improper to credit depreciation of that equipment to an operating appropriation that used the equipment to fill the customer's order.[55]

## 195. May every agency use the *Economy Act* to get reimbursed for any work it does for another agency?

Although the *Economy Act* is available to every federal agency as a vehicle to be reimbursed for providing goods or services to another agency, the authority is not unlimited. Agencies may not use the *Economy Act* to obtain reimbursement for a service that is a normal part of the providing agency's mission and for which it receives appropriations. For example:

- An agency acquiring land may not reimburse the Justice Department for the legal expenses incurred in the acquisition because these are the regular administrative expenses of the Justice Department for which it receives appropriations.
- Similarly, agencies may not reimburse the Treasury Department for the administrative expenses incurred in making disbursements on its behalf.
- Federal agencies may not reimburse the U.S. Patent and Trademark Office for services performed in administering the patent and trademark laws because the patent office is required by law to furnish these services and receives appropriations for them.
- The Library of Congress may not be reimbursed for recording assignments of copyrights to the United States.
- The Merit Systems Protection Board may not accept reimbursement from other federal agencies for the travel expenses of hearing officers to hearing sites away from the Board's regular field offices. The Board receives appropriations for such travel. Further, the inability of the Board's appropriation to fund such travel, whether due to inadequacy or exhaustion, does not permit another agency to pick up the costs.[56]

*Economy Act* orders tend to be voluntary, rather than mandatory, on the part of the providing agency. If the providing agency is required by law to perform a task and receives appropriations for it, then reimbursement would constitute improper augmentation of the providing agency's appropriation (as well as a purpose law violation on the part of the buying agency).

### 196. Are revolving funds exempt from the requirements of the miscellaneous receipts statute?

Revolving funds constitute a statutory exception to the miscellaneous receipts statute. Their receipts are credited directly to the fund and are available, without further appropriation by Congress, for expenditures to carry out the purposes of the fund.[57]

This does not mean, however, that 31 U.S.C. 3302(b) never applies to revolving funds. The statute that chartered the revolving fund specifies the receipts that may be credited to the fund. Receipts that are not related to the operation of the fund must be deposited in the Treasury as miscellaneous receipts.[58] A revolving fund established, for instance, to perform ship overhaul may not hold a bake sale or car wash to augment the fund. Only those receipts that relate to the statutory purpose of the revolving fund may be retained by the fund.

## GIFTS AND DONATIONS TO THE GOVERNMENT

### 197. May the federal government accept gifts from outside sources, or is that an improper augmentation of appropriations?

It has long been recognized that the United States may receive and accept gifts. No particular statutory authority is needed. A Supreme Court ruling stated: "Uninterrupted usage from the foundation of the Government has sanctioned it" (*United States v. Burnison*, 339 U.S. 87, 90 (1950)). The gifts may be of real or personal property and may be made by living persons or through the wills of deceased persons. Monetary gifts to the United States go to the general fund of the Treasury and present no augmentation problem because there is no appropriation to augment.[59]

## 198. May a federal agency also accept gifts?

Although gifts to the United States do not require statutory authority, gifts to an individual federal agency are viewed differently. The rule is that a government agency may not accept for its own use (that is, for retention by the agency or to credit its own appropriation) gifts of money or other property unless it has specific statutory authority to do so.[60]

Thus, the acceptance of a gift of money or other property by an agency lacking statutory authority to do so is an improper augmentation. If an agency does not have statutory authority to accept donations of money, it must turn the money in to the Treasury as miscellaneous receipts.[61]

Agencies without gift retention authority must report gifts of property to GSA, and the property will be treated in accordance with GSA regulations. Gifts from foreign governments or entities must also be reported to GSA and treated in accordance with 41 CFR 102.36.420 and part 101–49.[62]

## 199. Can agencies that have gift-receiving authority get around the miscellaneous receipts statute by classifying some of their receipts as gifts?

If a receipt does not meet the definition above, calling it a gift doesn't make it one. For example, in 25 Comp. Gen. 637, GAO held that a fee paid for the privilege of filming a motion picture in a national park is not a gift and must be deposited as miscellaneous receipts.[63]

## 200. May a federal employee accept travel-related promotional items?

Until 2001, the answer was "no." But on December 28, 2001, President Bush signed into law a provision allowing federal employees to retain travel-related promotional items for personal use (5 U.S.C. 5702). The law specifically states that a federal traveler who receives a promotional item (such as frequent flyer miles, upgrades, or access to carrier clubs or facilities) as a result of using travel or transportation services obtained at federal government expense may retain those items for personal use. The item must be obtained under the same terms as those offered to the general public and at no additional cost to the government. The Federal Travel Regulation addresses promotional items in 41 CFR 301-53 (2005).[64]

## *ANTIDEFICIENCY ACT* VIOLATION PENALTIES

### 201. What are the potential consequences or penalties if an employee violates the *Antideficiency Act*?

Violations of the *Antideficiency Act* are subject to penalties of two types—administrative and criminal. The *Antideficiency Act* is the only one of the 31 *United States Code* fiscal statutes to prescribe penalties of both types, which underscores congressional perception of the Act's importance.[65]

Sections 1349(a) and 1518 of Title 31 state that an officer or employee who violates 31 U.S.C. 1341(a), 1342, or 1517(a) "shall be subject to appropriate administrative discipline including, when circumstances warrant, suspension from duty without pay or removal from office." Employees have in fact been suspended, reduced in grade, or removed from government service for violating the Act.

In addition, per 31 U.S.C. 1350, an officer or employee who "knowingly and willfully" violates any of the three provisions cited above "shall be fined not more than $5,000, imprisoned for not more than 2 years, or both."

### 202. Could someone actually go to jail for using the wrong "color" of money—that is, for citing the wrong appropriation or overspending an apportionment when there is still money left in the appropriation?

Although the statute allows for criminal penalties, no case has been documented in which anyone has been prosecuted for, much less convicted of, a violation of the *Antideficiency Act*.

It is unlikely that the criminal penalties will ever be invoked, for two reasons. First, the Justice Department will not normally go after an individual unless he or she has personally benefited from the transaction that gave rise to the violation. Justice normally relies on the agency to take administrative action against the perpetrator. If personal gain was involved, other criminal statutes (theft, fraud, conspiracy) carry far greater penalties than the penalty for violating the *Antideficiency Act* (a $5,000 fine or two years imprisonment).

For example, the Army augmented its appropriation by more than $1 million in 2001 when it used unauthorized credits to fund various rehabilitation and refurbishment projects using contractor employees. The government official found responsible for the violation was prosecuted for felony theft of government property for submitting or approving more than $33,000 in fraudulent travel reimbursement claims. The official was fired and placed under house arrest for six months.

In an Army Corps of Engineers case, four employees used their government purchase cards to make $186,000 of personal nongovernment purchases—a violation of the *Antideficiency Act*. Two of the employees were dismissed from federal service. One was sentenced to six months in federal prison, and the other received three years of probation. It is unclear from the report under which law they were prosecuted, but it is unlikely that it was the *Antideficiency Act*.[66]

Even if someone were indicted for knowing and willful violation of the *Antideficiency Act*, it would be difficult to get a conviction. Convincing a jury of 12, most or all of whom have no knowledge of appropriations rules, that using the wrong appropriation or over-obligating an apportionment when the underlying appropriation had additional funds warrants a conviction and jail time would be virtually impossible.

Given that criminal prosecution is a remote possibility, the threat of significant administrative penalties is sufficient to evoke compliance with the law.

## 203. Can an *Antideficiency Act* violation be avoided by simply not recording some valid obligations, so that the accounting records don't show a shortage?

Posting an obligation to the accounting records merely evidences its existence. It does not create the obligation, and its absence in the records does not mean it does not exist. If obligations exceed budgetary authority, a violation has occurred, whether or not the accounting records are accurate.

Another caution here: The knowing or willful failure to record an obligation in order to conceal an *Antideficiency Act* violation is also a criminal offense![67]

## 204. Are the circumstances surrounding a violation (e.g., good faith, lack of intent, minor nature of the violation, inadequate training) ever relevant in determining whether a violation has occurred and whether it should be reported?

All of those circumstances are irrelevant in determining whether a violation has occurred. Further, violations that occur are to be reported. However, these circumstances are usually relevant when assessing penalties against the violator. Such factors as intent, state of mind, workload, and lack of training or effective supervision may all be considered when the agency imposes its administrative sanctions.[68]

# AGENCY REPORTING PROCEDURES

## 205. What must an agency do if it has violated the *Antideficiency Act*?

The first step is to determine whether a violation has actually occurred. In some cases—for example, purchasing a prohibited item for which there is no appropriation available—it is obvious that a violation has occurred. Not every situation is so clear-cut, however. For example, if your accounting records indicate that you over-obligated your apportionment by several thousand dollars during a particular period, the prudent course of action is to review the obligations recorded in the records to ensure they are in fact valid obligations and were actually obligated during the period of apparent shortfall. It is not uncommon for obligations to be posted before they are true obligations, and the level of obligations is often overstated. Refer to 31 U.S.C. 1501 for guidance in determining whether the documentary evidence requirement for obligations has been met.

Agencies often have their own regulations detailing the process to follow when a violation is suspected. This may entail appointing a preliminary investigating official to determine whether a violation has occurred.

## 206. Assuming the agency has determined that a violation of the *Antideficiency Act* occurred, what is the next step?

Sections 1351 and 1517(b) of Title 31 require the agency head to "report immediately to the president and Congress all relevant facts and a statement of actions taken." The reports are to be signed by the agency head, and the report to the President is to be forwarded through the director of OMB. Further, the *Consolidated Appropriations Act* for 2005 amended the *Antideficiency Act* to add that the heads of executive branch agencies and the mayor of the District of Columbia must also transmit a copy of each report to the comptroller general on the same date the report is transmitted to the President and Congress.[69] GAO then publishes an annual summary of all reports received.

## 207. Can the person named as the violator ask the comptroller general or the courts for relief from the violation?

Unlike pecuniary liability against an accountable officer, for which there is potential relief available from the comptroller general, the courts have ruled (*Thurston v. United States*, 696 F. Supp. 680 (D.D.C. 1988)) that there is no private right of action for declaratory, mandatory, or injunctive relief under the *Antideficiency Act*.[70] The violation either happened or it didn't. If it happened, the facts are reported. No relief is available.

## 208. What happens if OMB suspects an *Antideficiency Act* violation?

Whenever OMB determines that a violation of the *Antideficiency Act* might have occurred, it may request that an investigation or audit be undertaken or conducted by the agency. In such cases, a report describing the results of the investigation or audit will be submitted to OMB through the head of the agency. If the report indicates that no violation of the *Antideficiency Act* has occurred, the agency head will so inform OMB and forward a copy of the report to OMB. If the report indicates that a violation of the *Antideficiency Act* has occurred, the agency head will report to the President, Congress, and the Comptroller General as soon as possible.[71]

## 209. What happens if GAO reports a violation in one of its audits or reports?

Violations reported by GAO in connection with audits and investigations must be reported to the President, Congress, and the Comptroller General in the same manner as described above. In these cases, the report to the President will indicate whether the agency agrees that a violation has occurred, and if so, it will explain why the violation was not discovered and previously reported by the agency.[72]

## 210. What if the agency disagrees with GAO's finding regarding a violation?

If the agency does not agree that a violation has occurred, the report of violation must still be made to the President, Congress, and the Comptroller General, but it will explain the agency's position.[73]

## 211. What happens if the agency not only disagrees with GAO's finding but also does not send in a report of violation?

Should an agency fail to make the required report within a reasonable period of time, GAO will advise Congress that the agency violated the *Antideficiency Act* but has not yet reported the violation. For example, GAO advised Congress that the Department of Energy had violated the *Antideficiency Act* in fiscal years 2006 and 2007 but had not reported the violations to Congress more than six months after GAO found the violations. Subsequently, two months after GAO notified Congress, the department made the required reports and provided copies to GAO.[74]

## ANALYSIS OF *ANTIDEFICIENCY ACT* REPORTS[75]

### 212. How many violations were reported during the period 2005–2011?

A total of 141 reports were submitted. A few of the reports consolidated multiple dissimilar violations into one report, so there were actually 147 violations reported. Several reports cover multiple violations of a similar nature that occurred in the same time frame or were of a continuous nature. I have counted those reports as containing just one violation per report. For example, the Selective Service System consolidated 14 similar *bona fide* needs rule violations that occurred within a six-week period into one report. This counts as one violation in the following statistics.

### 213. Which agency had the most violations during the period 2005–2011?

The number of violations reported by each agency is shown in Figure 4-1. The U.S. Army had by far the most violations, with 46. Collectively, DoD had 95, which represents 65 percent of all violations reported.

### 214. What was the nature of the violations during the period 2005–2011?

Figure 4-2 shows the types of violations reported.

There were 62 purpose law violations (42 percent of all violations). They are broken down into two categories—using the wrong appropriation for a lawful purpose and using any appropriation for an unlawful purpose (improper purchases). In the former category (38 violations), the wrong appropriation was cited at the time of the transaction, and when a correction to the accounting records was made at a later date, it was found that insufficient funds had been continuously available in the proper appropriation, resulting in an *Antideficiency Act* violation. There were 24 violations in the improper purchases category. These

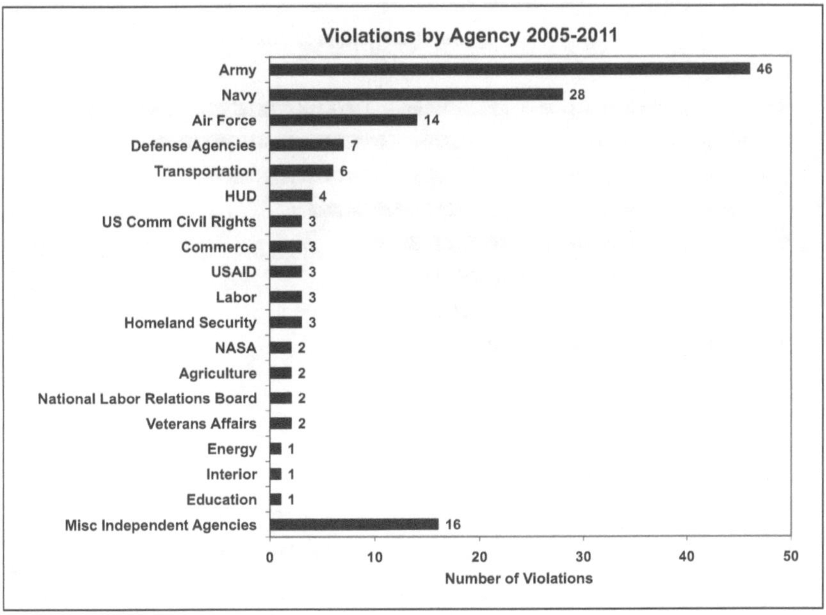


**Figure 4-1:** Violations by Agency 2005-2011.

were purchases made for items for which there was no legally available appropriation. These purpose law violations are automatic violations of the *Antideficiency Act.*

In 33 of the violations, the agency simply over-obligated or over-disbursed its appropriation or apportionment. These violations resulted from myriad circumstances, ranging from financial systems failure to confusion following 9/11 to failure to post obligations in a timely manner.

Another major cause of reported violations involved obligating or expending funds in advance of an appropriation or apportionment. There were 17 such violations. Similar in nature are *bona fide* needs rule violations, in that they involve obligating current funds for future years' requirements. Twelve *bona fide* needs violations occurred.

The three broad categories just mentioned—purpose law violations, exhausting an appropriation or apportionment, and obligating in

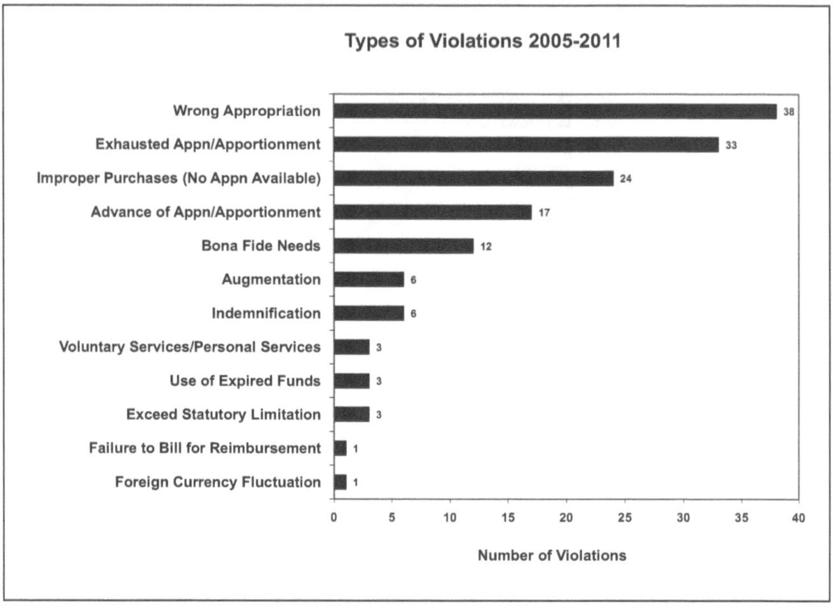


**Figure 4-2:** Types of Violations 2005-2011.

advance of an appropriation or a *bona fide* need—accounted for 84 percent of all reported violations.

## 215. How were violators during the period 2005–2011 disciplined?

Figure 4-3 shows the types of action the agencies took against the violators. The 147 violation reports identified 300 responsible individuals. The total number of disciplinary actions shown totals 307 because a few individuals were disciplined in more than one way.

In 128 (42 percent) of the cases, no discipline was taken, either because the employee had already left federal service (80 individuals, or 26 percent) or because the agency determined that no discipline was warranted due to the circumstances of the violation (48 cases, or 16 percent).

Oral and written reprimands, counseling, cautions, and admonitions collectively constituted 139 (45 percent) of all disciplinary actions.

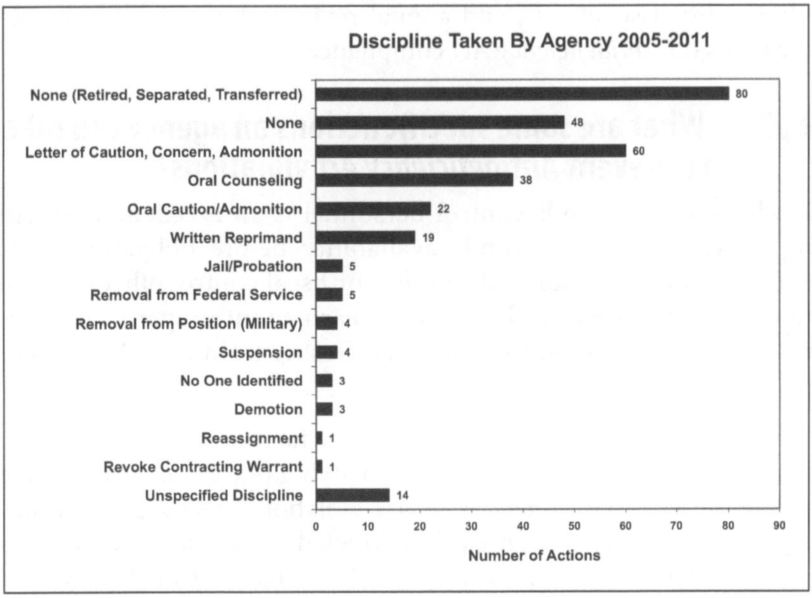


**Figure 4-3:** Discipline Taken By Agency 2005-2011.

Five civilians lost their federal positions, and four military members were removed from their positions.

Fourteen of the reports indicated that discipline was taken, but the nature of that discipline was not reported.

## PREVENTING VIOLATIONS OF THE *ANTIDEFICIENCY ACT*

### 216. How can I ensure my organization doesn't incur any *Antideficiency Act* violations?

While there is no way to be absolutely certain a violation will not occur, there are a number of actions you can take to minimize the likelihood of a violation. Many fall under the umbrella of internal controls. You should have a robust internal control program that complies with the GAO Standards for Internal Control, OMB Circular A-123, and your own agency regulations. Your internal control risk assessments, vulnerability assessments, and annual reviews should include a specific focus on *Antideficiency Act* compliance.

## 217. What are some specific actions an agency can take to prevent *Antideficiency Act* violations?

Good training of funds control personnel is an excellent start. All employees who certify funds availability before obligation (e.g., those who work in your budget office or fiscal control office) should attend an appropriations law class to learn about proper use of federal funds. They should then attend refresher training at least every five years.

Certifying officers, who certify vouchers for payment, should also attend appropriations law training. Certifying officers are the last line of defense against *Antideficiency Act* violations. Many purpose law violations could have been easily corrected—and *Antideficiency Act* violations avoided—if the certifying officers had not made incorrect payments.

It is important for funds holders to read the agency's appropriations act each year. You will find your agency's appropriations act at http://thomas.loc.gov. You should read not only the actual appropriation language to ascertain the current year purpose, time, amount, and earmarks, but also any general, administrative, or special provisions that apply to your agency. Often, these additional provisions are physically separated by many pages from your actual appropriation, so you must carefully look for them. These provisions often contain specific authorizations and prohibitions as well as additional earmarks. Violating one of the provisions might well result in an *Antideficiency Act* violation.

GAO's daily email service is another good source of information. Subscribers receive all newly published comptroller general decisions. The emails help keep you informed about any changes in the rules on the proper use of federal funds. Go to http://www.gao.gov/subscribe/index.php to sign up for this free service.

You should also review the GAO database of *Antideficiency Act* violations (http://www.gao.gov/ada/antideficiencyrpts.htm) when it is published each year. Pay attention to the violations related to the kinds of transactions your agency processes. Critically reviewing the database might help you to avoid similar violations.

## 218. What can I do from an operational standpoint to help avoid violations?

Follow these guidelines:

- First and foremost, stress to all personnel the importance of promptly and accurately recording all obligations. Delay in posting obligations to accounting records is the root cause of many violations because the available balances are overstated until the accounting catches up with the obligations. If your agency does commitment accounting, it is also important to immediately post all commitments as soon as the availability of funds has been certified. If your agency does not use commitment accounting, consider it.
- Make certain at the beginning of each fiscal year and each quarter that you have a valid funding document authorizing your obligation authority before certifying any funds for obligation. Many reported *Antideficiency Act* violations have occurred during periods covered by continuing resolutions; the agencies had not yet received apportionments from OMB. Do not assume that apportionment is automatic. It isn't.
- Question transactions that are unusual or just don't look right. A large percentage of reported *Antideficiency Act* violations resulted from the purchase of unauthorized items. Be especially wary of requests for items you've never bought before. Keep in mind the prohibitions against buying food, gifts, and other personal items.
- If you have doubts about a transaction, resist pressure from above for immediate action. Make sure that a transaction is proper before authorizing it, no matter how much pressure your boss might apply. If the transaction is not proper, say so, and don't certify it. Remember, the person who is the funds holder and certifies the transaction—not the person who requested it—is the one normally held responsible for a violation. Don't automatically assume the boss is right.

- Periodically remind all managers of the prohibition against accepting voluntary services. Employees who are entitled to compensation for overtime work must receive it in the form of pay or compensatory time off. Managers must be aware that they may not suffer or permit their employees to voluntarily give up their entitlement to compensation.
- Make friends with your agency's legal counsel. Developing good rapport with the attorneys will help you get quick and thoughtful responses to your questions. Make sure at least one of the attorneys has some expertise in appropriations law. If none do, gently suggest some training so that your legal office can give you the assistance you need and deserve. If you are sponsoring appropriations law training for your financial personnel, offer one or more slots to your legal office.

## 219. What might be agencies' greatest area of vulnerability to *Antideficiency Act* violations in the future?

The use of government purchase cards and government travel cards has exploded recently, and it is likely that many violations will result. Nonfinancial and non-contracting personnel use purchase cards and travel cards to obligate the government and approve payments. Thousands of people in every organization, not just a relative few, now certify funds availability. Most of these cardholders and approvers have not been trained in appropriations law and are unaware of the *Antideficiency Act*. Auditors will certainly find numerous violations as they increase their surveillance of purchase-card use.

In addition, GAO stated in a recent decision[76] that purchase-card approving officials will be burdened with pecuniary liability for any payments made for unauthorized items. Such officials could suffer a double whammy—being named in an *Antideficiency Act* violation report and possibly disciplined, then being forced to pay for the unauthorized purchases out of their own pockets.

To avoid problems, agencies need strong internal controls over their cards. In January 2009 OMB published a revised appendix (appendix B) to its Circular A-123 that makes recommendations for controlling the use of government purchase cards and travel cards. The appendix lists specific requirements agencies should include in their systems of internal controls for managing charge card programs. Strict compliance with appendix B will substantially reduce your risk of incurring *Antideficiency Act* violations as a result of misuse of government charge cards. Go to http://www.whitehouse.gov/omb/circulars/a123/a123 _appendix_b.pdf to review this directive.

## NOTES

1. U.S. Government Accountability Office, *Principles of Federal Appropriations Law, Volume II* (GAO-06-382SP), February 2006, Chap. 6, 6-6.
2. Ibid., 6-7.
3. Ibid., 6-5.
4. Ibid., 6-26.
5. Ibid.
6. Ibid., 6-24.
7. Ibid., 6-37.
8. Ibid., 6-36.
9. Ibid., 6-38.
10. Ibid., 6-40.
11. Ibid.
12. Ibid., 6-41.
13. Ibid., 6-46.
14. Ibid., 6-47.
15. Ibid., 6-59.
16. Ibid., 6-60.
17. Ibid., 6-80.
18. Ibid.
19. Ibid.
20. U.S Government Accountability Office, *Antideficiency Act Reports – Fiscal Year 2007,* ADA-07-08.
21. Public Law 110-161, Division B. Title V.
22. U.S. Government Accountability Office, *Principles,* Chap. 6, 6-82.

23. Ibid., 6-83.
24. Ibid., 6-88.
25. Ibid.
26. Ibid., 6-116.
27. Ibid., 6-118.
28. U.S. Office of Management and Budget Circular A-11, Section 145.2.
29. U.S. Government Accountability Office, *Principles,* Chap. 6, 6-95.
30. Ibid., 6-95.
31. 30 Op. Att'y Gen. 51 (1913).
32. 27 Comp. Dec. 131, 132-33 (1920).
33. U.S. Government Accountability Office, *Principles,* Chap. 6, 6-97.
34. U.S Government Accountability Office, *Antideficiency Act Reports – Fiscal Year 2005,* ADA-05-13.
35. U.S. Government Accountability Office, *Principles,* Chap. 6, 6-163.
36. Ibid., 6-163.
37. Ibid.
38. Ibid., 6-164.
39. Ibid., 6-166.
40. Ibid., 6-167.
41. Ibid., 6-168.
42. Ibid., 6-169.
43. Ibid., 6-170.
44. Ibid.
45. Ibid.
46. Ibid., 6-194.
47. U.S. Government Accountability Office decision, B-302962 (June 10, 2005).
48. U.S. Government Accountability Office, *Principles,* Chap. 6, 6-195.
49. Ibid., 6-197.
50. U.S. Government Accountability Office decision, B-302962.
51. U.S. Government Accountability Office, *Principles,* Chap. 6, 6-199.
52. 4B Op. Off. Legal Counsel 684, 687 (1980).
53. U.S. Government Accountability Office, *Principles,* Chap. 6, 6-211.
54. Ibid., 6-202.

55. Ibid.
56. Ibid., 6-237.
57. Ibid., 6-206.
58. Ibid.
59. Ibid., 6-222.
60. Ibid.
61. Ibid., 6-223.
62. Ibid.
63. Ibid.
64. Ibid., 6-234.
65. Ibid., 6-143.
66. U.S Government Accountability Office, *Antideficiency Act Reports – Fiscal Year 2007,* ADA-07-03 and ADA-07-13.
67. U.S. Government Accountability Office, *Principles,* Chap. 6, 6-144.
68. Ibid., 6-144.
69. Ibid.
70. Ibid., 6-145.
71. U.S. Office of Management and Budget, Circular A-11, Section 145.9.
72. Ibid., Section 145.8.
73. Ibid.
74. U.S Government Accountability Office, *Antideficiency Act Reports – Fiscal Year 2008,* ADA-08-05.
75. All the material in this Analysis section is based on the *Antideficiency Act Reports* databases published by the U.S. Government Accountability Office for fiscal years 2005 through 2008. The reports are available at http://www.gao.gov/ada/antideficiencyrpts.htm.
76. U.S. Government Accountability Office decision, B-307693 (April 12, 2007).

# Chapter 5
# Obligation of Appropriations

When people first come to the federal government as employees, they normally have a difficult time understanding, let alone accepting, the way the government controls its spending. Unlike the private sector or state and local governments that keep track of assets, liabilities, and net worth (or net position in the government setting), the federal government uses a separate set of accounts for budgetary control. These accounts track and control the use of budgetary authority, as well as the status of that authority, mostly by tracking and controlling obligations. The concept of obligation control is central to federal operations.

The previous chapter stated that *Antideficiency Act* violations can be incurred by obligating in advance or in excess of an appropriation or apportionment. What if an agency's accounting records show it to be overobligated? Does it automatically begin its *Antideficiency Act* violation report? Of course not. The first thing to do is determine whether a violation actually occurred. One of the steps in that investigation is to examine recorded obligations to see if they are recorded at the right amount and if all the recorded obligations are, in fact, really obligations. To perform that task, one must understand the nature of obligations and know, for various commodities and transactions, what constitutes an obligation, what its proper amount is, and when it exists. This chapter answers all of those questions.

# THE NATURE OF OBLIGATIONS

## 220. Just what is an obligation?

In the most general terms, an *obligation* is a "definite commitment which creates a legal liability of the Government for the payment of appropriated funds for goods and services ordered or received." GAO has stressed that obligations must be "definite and certain."[1]

Restating the definition, an obligation is some action that creates a legal liability on the part of the government to make payment. Payment may occur at the time of obligation or in the future.

The term *obligation* includes both matured and unmatured commitments. A matured commitment* is a legal liability that is currently payable; for example, goods ordered have been received and accepted. An unmatured commitment is a liability that is not yet payable but for which a definite commitment exists; for example, the liability for future monthly rental payments under a lease. Both types of liability are obligations. The fact that an unmatured liability may be subject to a right of cancellation does not negate the obligation.[2]

The main difference between an obligation in budgetary accounting and a liability in financial accounting is that an obligation occurs when an item is ordered, whereas in financial accounting a liability doesn't exist until the item is delivered. But this is a significant difference because the government's budget authority is considered to be legally encumbered at the point of obligation. It is obligations that drive *Antideficiency Act* implications.

* In this discussion, the use of the word *commitment* to help describe an obligation is different from the classic definition of *commitment* in budgetary accounting where it means an administrative reservation of funds that is *not* an obligation. This use of *commitment* is from its everyday meaning, "an agreement, promise, or pledge to do something."

## CRITERIA FOR RECORDING OBLIGATIONS

### 221. Where would I find the criteria for recording obligations for various commodities and transactions? What constitutes the obligation, how much is it, and when does it occur?

The standards for the proper recording of obligations are provided at 31 U.S.C. 1501(a). This section was enacted because congressional committees were receiving unreliable and inconsistent budget review figures from the agencies, in large part because of the lack of clearly defined standards for recording obligations. The primary purpose of this statute is to ensure that agencies record only those transactions that meet specified standards for legitimate obligations.[3]

Section 1501 begins by stating that "an amount shall be recorded as an obligation of the United States Government only when supported by documentary evidence," and then it proceeds to specify nine criteria for recording obligations. If a given transaction does not meet any of the nine criteria, it is not an obligation and may not be recorded as one.

It is also important to distinguish the difference between the existence of an obligation and the act of recording an obligation. Recording merely evidences the obligation; it does not create it. If a transaction does not meet the standard to constitute an obligation, recording it will not make it an obligation. Conversely, failing to record a valid obligation in no way diminishes its validity or affects the fiscal year to which it is properly chargeable.[4]

### 222. What are the nine standards for obligations?

The nine standards, listed below, are at 31 U.S.C. 1501 (a), subsections (1) through (9).

1. Contracts
2. Loans
3. Interagency Orders Required by Law
4. Orders without Advertising

5. Grants and Subsidies
6. Pending Litigation
7. Employment and Travel
8. Public Utilities
9. Other Legal Liabilities (anything that doesn't fit the first eight).

## Contracts

### 223. Can you elaborate on any of the standards for obligations?

The world of contracts is high-dollar, broad, complex, and subject to error when recording obligations. So let's look at the criteria for contracts first.

Subsection (a)(1) of 31 U.S.C. 1501 establishes the minimum requirements for recording obligations for contracts. It states there must be documentary evidence of:

> (1) a binding agreement between an agency and another person (including an agency) that is –
>
> (A) in writing, in a way and form, and for a purpose authorized by law; and
>
> (B) executed before the end of the period of availability for obligation of the appropriation or fund used for specific goods to be delivered, real property to be bought or leased, or work or service to be provided.[5]

Summarizing, this subsection imposes all the following requirements for a valid contract:

1. A binding agreement
2. In writing
3. For a purpose authorized by law

4. Executed before the expiration of the period of obligational availability (and, as we saw in Chapter 3, meets a *bona fide* need of that fiscal year)
5. Calls for *specific* goods, real property, work, or services.

If a transaction doesn't meet all of these criteria, it isn't a valid contract. If it isn't a contract, it isn't an obligation, and if it isn't an obligation, it shouldn't be paid.

## 224. The first four criteria for a valid contract are pretty clear, but what does "specific" goods or services mean?

The statute requires documentary evidence of a binding agreement for specific goods or services.[6] An agreement that fails this test is not a valid obligation. For example, in an effort to use expiring funds, an agency might send a purchase order to a local sign shop asking for "regulatory, warning, and guide signs based on information supplied" on requisitions to be issued in the future. This purchase order does not obligate agency funds because the description is inadequate for the vendor to begin work. He doesn't know how many signs, how big, what color, or what they are to say. If the requisitions are sent to the vendor after the close of the fiscal year, they become an obligation of the new fiscal year because no obligation existed in the previous year.

Audit reports show that hundreds of millions of dollars of orders were sent to various working capital funds at the end of FY 2004 and 2005 that lacked the required specificity to constitute obligations. The agencies sending the orders were accused of attempting to "park" their funds with another agency to keep them from expiring. The fallout was the loss of the funds in the expiring year, multiple audit findings, congressional interest and intervention, and changes in policy.

## 225. Requirements, indefinite-quantity, and indefinite-delivery, indefinite-quantity (IDIQ) contracts are not specific as to quantity and the timing of delivery. Does that mean they are not obligations?

First, some definitions:

- A *requirements contract* is one where the government agrees to purchase all of a particular item or service from a given contractor, and the contractor agrees to fill all requirements.[7]
- An *indefinite-quantity contract* is one where the contractor agrees to supply the quantities ordered by the government, but the government is free to go elsewhere for the rest of its requirements.[8]
- An *indefinite-delivery, indefinite-quantity (IDIQ)* contract is a form of indefinite-quantity contract in which actual delivery dates are undefined at the time of contract award.[9]

Under any of these types of contracts, the government orders specific quantities from time to time by issuing a document—called by various names, such as work order, task order, or delivery order.

In a requirements contract the government must state a realistic estimated total quantity. The contract may place a minimum amount to be ordered and a maximum limit, but that is not required.[10] Requirements contracts may be issued with no minimums. If the requirements don't materialize and nothing is ordered, the government has no obligation. Thus, at the time of the award of a no-minimum requirements contract, no obligation would be recorded in the records because none exists. If the contract calls for a minimum quantity, the minimum amount is an obligation at the time of contract award.[11]

Indefinite-quantity contracts (and IDIQs) must include a minimum purchase requirement, which must be more than nominal. The amount of the minimum purchase is recorded as an obligation at the time of contract award.[12]

Summarizing the obligational impact for all of these kinds of variable-quantity contracts:

1. Any required minimum purchase must be obligated when the contract is awarded.

2. Subsequent obligations occur as work orders or delivery orders are placed and are chargeable to the fiscal year in which the order is placed.

### 226. Determining how much to record as the obligation is sometimes difficult. It's easy if the contract is firm fixed-price. But cost-reimbursable contracts and fixed-price contracts with escalation clauses or incentive provisions are not always clear. How much should be recorded as the obligation when the final amount is unknown?

For fixed-price contracts with escalation, price redetermination, or incentive provisions, the initial obligation to be recorded is the fixed price or target price for incentive clause contracts.[13] If the target price in an incentive contract is $20 million, with a ceiling price of $25 million, the proper amount to record is the target price of $20 million. As time passes and it becomes known whether the incentive will be earned (or prices revised under price redeterminations), the value of the obligation needs to be adjusted to reflect the best evidence available. To avoid possible *Antideficiency Act* problems, most agencies have regulations that provide for the administrative reservation of funds (a commitment) to cover the additional potential liability.

For cost-reimbursable contracts, record the amount that reflects the best cost estimate at the time. Do not record at the maximum possible amount. Such contracts must be closely monitored and the level of obligations adjusted as new information becomes available.

## *Interagency Transactions*

### 227. Are the rules for obligations in connection with interagency transactions the same as those for contracts?

Section 1501 of 31 U.S.C. addresses interagency transactions in two places. Interagency transactions required by law are covered in a separate section of the code; those not required by law, usually referred to as "voluntary orders," are covered under the same section as contracts. Thus, voluntary orders are recorded in the same manner as contracts, but the authority that governs the particular interagency transaction, not contract practices, determines the obligational treatment of a voluntary order.[14] There are four aspects of voluntary orders to consider when determining what constitutes an obligation and when it occurs under such interagency orders: (1) *Economy Act* agreements, (2) non-*Economy Act* agreements, (3) orders from stock, and (4) project orders.

Let's discuss each of these four aspects before going on to interagency orders required by law.

## 228. What is the *Economy Act* and how are obligations under it handled?

A detailed discussion of interagency transactions and the *Economy Act* is presented in Chapter 6, Intragovernmental Transactions. However, a brief explanation follows.

The *Economy Act* is an exception to the Miscellaneous Receipts statute, discussed in the previous chapter. The Economy Act allows a federal agency to perform work for another agency and be reimbursed for it. It allows the reimbursement to be credited to the performing activity's appropriation, rather than being sent to Treasury as a miscellaneous receipt. Without the *Economy Act*, or other similar statutes, the whole concept of reimbursements would be impossible.

An *Economy Act* agreement is recorded as an obligation at the time the two parties reach a "binding agreement."[15] This normally occurs when the performing agency accepts the order from the ordering agency.

However, *Economy Act* agreements are subject to one additional requirement. If a fixed-year appropriation is used for the order, the ordering agency must deobligate the obligation at the end of the fiscal year to the extent that the performing agency has not incurred an obligation. In other words, if the performing agency has not (1) provided the requested item to the ordering agency, (2) performed the requested service, or (3) entered into a valid contract with another person to provide the requested item or service to the ordering agency by September 30, the funds must be deobligated.[16]

For example, if a performing agency's employee is painting a room for the customer at an agreed price of $1000 and finishes only half the room by September 30, the ordering agency would have to deobligate $500. If it wants the room finished, a new agreement for the remaining work ($500) would need to be executed in the new fiscal year.

## 229. What are non-*Economy Act* agreements and how are those obligations recorded?

Agreements that cite some authority other than the *Economy Act* are recorded in virtually the same manner as contracts with the private sector. The deobligation requirements of the *Economy Act* do not apply, and so long as the agreement was finalized during the period of availability and the *bona fide* needs rule is satisfied, the entire level of effort is funded from the appropriation current at the time of the agreement between the parties.[17]

It is therefore necessary to determine the specific statutory authority that allows the interagency agreement in order to properly obligate the ordering agency's funds.

## 230. The third aspect of voluntary orders was "orders from stock." What does that mean?

The terms means that the supplying agency has the item in stock (on hand) or routinely on order. An order for items to be delivered from stock is a recordable obligation if (1) it is intended to meet a *bona fide* need of the fiscal year in which the order is placed or to replace stock used in that fiscal year and (2) the order is firm and complete. Firm and complete means the order requests prompt delivery of specific available stock items for a stated cost and must be accepted in writing by the supplying agency.[18]

Materials manufactured for a particular order are not "stock" materials. Likewise, an item not stocked by the supplying agency is not a recordable obligation until that agency purchases the item or executes a contract for it.[19]

## 231. Finally, what is a "project order"?

Project orders are orders made under the authority of 41 U.S.C. 23 (or 14 U.S.C. 151 for the Coast Guard), which relate to military projects. They apply only to transactions between the military departments and defense agencies—in other words, internal to DoD. The authority is used for non-severable services or the manufacture or overhaul of supplies or equipment. It may not be used for replenishing stock. The requirement of specificity applies to project orders.[20]

Because a project order is not an *Economy Act* transaction, the deobligation requirement of the *Economy Act* does not apply.

## 232. Now that we've covered voluntary orders, what interagency transactions are required by law?

Some interagency transactions are required by statute to be placed with a particular supplying agency. Such orders are not *Economy Act* transactions, and the deobligation requirement does not apply.

These interagency transactions are recorded as obligations at the time they are placed. So long as the *bona fide* needs rule is met, it doesn't matter if the work will be performed in the following fiscal year.[21]

Examples of interagency transactions required by law are printing and binding services provided by the Government Printing Office and building alteration, management, and related services performed by the General Services Administration.

### *Grants*

## 233. What constitutes an obligation when grant funds are used, and when does the obligation occur?

To properly obligate an appropriation for an assistance program, some action creating a definite liability against the appropriation must occur during the period of obligational availability of the appropriation. Normally, this involves a discretionary action by an agency of awarding a grant that is evidenced by a grant agreement. The document itself may vary by agency and may be in the form of an agency's approval of a grant application or a letter of commitment to the grantee. There must be some action to establish a firm commitment on the part of the government, and it must be unconditional. The award terms must be communicated to the grantee, and if any prerequisites exist, such as putting up matching funds, the prerequisites must also be accepted by the grantee during the period of availability of the grant funds.[22]

Once the appropriation has been properly obligated, performance by the grantee and actual disbursement of funds may extend beyond the period of availability.

## *Employment*

### 234. What does 31 U.S.C. 1501 have to say about employment—salaries and related expenses?

Employment and travel are covered under subsection 1501(a)(7). Salaries of government employees, as well as related items such as employee benefits, are obligations at the time the salaries are earned, that is, when the services are rendered.[23]

Annual leave obligates appropriations at the time it is taken.[24]

Incentive or performance awards are obligations at the time the awards are made, meaning the time at which the administration determination to make the award is approved.[25]

Severance pay is obligated on a pay period-by-pay period basis. If the severance payments cross fiscal years, the obligations are charged to the separate fiscal years.[26]

Uniform allowances become obligations when the employee incurs the expense of an agency-prescribed uniform and becomes entitled to reimbursement.[27]

## *Travel*

### 235. How are travel expenses treated?

The basic rule on temporary duty travel is that obligations are created when the travel is actually performed. The issuance of a travel order in itself does not constitute a contractual obligation. It is merely an authorization for the person specified to incur an obligation. Temporary duty travel expenses are chargeable to the fiscal year or years in which they are actually incurred.[28]

Where tickets are purchased in one fiscal year and the travel begins in the following fiscal year, the obligation is chargeable to the year in which the travel is performed even though early purchase of the tickets might have been necessary to ensure reservations. However, the entire costs of round-trip tickets are chargeable to the fiscal year in which they are purchased, so long as the travel begins in that fiscal year.[29]

Per diem accrues from day to day. Thus, when travel begins in one fiscal year and ends in the next, the per diem obligation is split between the fiscal years.[30]

When the employee is transferred to a new duty station, the obligations are handled differently from temporary duty travel. The rule is that all reimbursable travel and transportation expenses of a transferred employee are recorded as obligations against the appropriation current when the employee is issued travel orders.[31]

## CONTINGENT LIABILITIES

### 236. What is a contingent liability, and how is it recorded in accounting records?

A contingent liability is fundamentally different from an obligation. While an obligation is a definite liability, a contingent liability does not create an obligation unless and until some contingency materializes. GAO defines it as "an existing condition, situation, or set of circumstances that poses the *possibility* of a loss to an agency that will ultimately be resolved when one or more events occur or fail to occur." Contingent liabilities are not recordable as obligations; they become obligations only if and when the contingency materializes.[32]

Although contingent liabilities are not recorded as obligations, sound financial management practices require that agencies recognize them.

The normal process is to carry them as administrative reservations of funds, or commitments, until the contingency is known.

Contingent liabilities may also be sufficiently important to warrant their recognition in a footnote in agency financial statements.

## NOTES

1. U.S. Government Accountability Office, *Principles,* Chap. 7, 7-3.
2. Ibid., 7-4.
3. Ibid., 7-7.
4. Ibid., 7-8.
5. Ibid., 7-10.
6. Ibid., 7-17.
7. Ibid., 7-19.
8. Ibid.
9. Ibid., 7-20.
10. Ibid., 7-19.
11. Ibid., 7-21.
12. Ibid., 7-20.
13. Ibid., 7-24.
14. Ibid., 7-29.
15. Ibid.
16. Ibid.
17. Ibid. 7-30.
18. Ibid., 7-33.
19. Ibid.
20. Ibid., 7-34.
21. Ibid., 7-37.
22. Ibid., 7-40.
23. Ibid., 7-46.
24. Ibid., 7-47.
25. Ibid.
26. Ibid.
27. Ibid., 7-49.

28. Ibid., 7-50.
29. Ibid.
30. Ibid.
31. Ibid., 7-52.
32. Ibid., 7-56.

# Chapter 6

# Intragovernmental Transactions

Although most financial transactions conducted by the federal government are with external parties, a significant number are within or between government agencies. These are called intragovernmental or interagency transactions, and there are special rules on the use of government funds when engaging in such transactions. There are two broad categories of interagency transactions—reimbursements and revolving funds. This chapter explores the acquisition of goods or services through the process of reimbursable orders and revolving fund activities.

## 237. Why are special rules needed for reimbursements and revolving funds?

In 1932, as part of a package of measures designed to reduce government spending and help the nation to fight its way out of the Great Depression, Congress enacted the first government-wide statutory authority for federal agencies to provide work, services, or materials to other federal agencies on a reimbursable basis.[1] That was the beginning of the *Economy Act*. Prior to this statute, despite the obvious advantages of interagency dealings, agencies' hands were tied by the purpose law and the miscellaneous receipts statute, previously discussed. The purpose law limits the use of appropriations to the purposes intended by Congress. Therefore, an agency could not use its appropriation to do work to benefit another agency. Further, even if an agency did have statutory language allowing the use of its appropriation for another agency, the miscellaneous receipts statute mandated that any reimbursement collected must be deposited in Treasury. Thus, without the legislative relief provided by the *Economy Act*, the whole concept of reimbursable work as we know it today just didn't exist.

## REIMBURSEMENTS

### Economy Act *Orders and Non*-Economy Act *Orders*

#### 238. So the *Economy Act* is the basic authority for one agency to do work for another and get paid for it?

Correct. A House committee report summarized the purpose of the *Economy Act*:

> The purpose of this bill is to permit the utilization of the materials, supplies, facilities, and personnel belonging to one department by another department or independent establishment which is not equipped to furnish the materials, work, or services for itself, and to provide a uniform procedure so far as practicable for all departments.
>
> Your committee also believes that very substantial economies can be realized by one department availing itself of the equipment and services of another department in proper cases. A free interchange of work as contemplated by this bill will enable all bureaus and activities of the Government to be utilized to their fullest and in many cases make it unnecessary for departments to set up duplicating and overlapping activities of their own.[2]

#### 239. Where do I find the *Economy Act* in the *United States Code*, and what exactly does it say?

The basic authority is found in 31 U.S.C. 1535. Subsection (a) specifies four conditions that must be met, as follows:[3]

> (a) The head of an agency or major organizational unit within an agency may place an order with a major organizational unit within the same agency or another agency for goods or services if –

(1) amounts are available;

(2) the head of the ordering agency or unit decides the order is in the best interest of the United States government;

(3) the agency or unit to fill the order is able to provide or get by contract the ordered goods or services; and

(4) the head of the agency decides ordered goods or services cannot be provided by contract as conveniently or cheaply by a commercial enterprise.

These four numbered sections prescribe the basic conditions that dictate the use of the *Economy Act*. There are other provisions on who can use the authority and what it may be used for; they will be discussed later.

## 240. Can you discuss those four conditions in more detail?

Let's take each of them in turn:

**(1) Funds available.** This first condition goes directly to the purpose law, 31 U.S.C. 1301(a). The ordering agency must have funds that are available for the contemplated purpose. In other words, the purpose of the transaction must be something the ordering agency is authorized to do. The *Economy Act*, or, in fact, any other act providing transfer authority, does not authorize an agency to use another agency to do anything it could not lawfully do itself. The ordering agency does not need specific authority in its appropriation language to use the *Economy Act*, but of course it must adhere to any monetary limits Congress might choose to impose.[4]

**(2) Best interest of the government.** The second condition is that the head of the ordering agency must determine that the order is in the best interest of the government. This condition creates little impediment because there is no case law where this provision has been applied.[5]

**(3) Performing agency's "position."** This condition—the agency is "able to provide" the goods or services—means the performing agency must be "in a position to supply or equipped to render" the materials or services needed. This requirement goes to the heart of the *Economy Act*. The objective of the statute is to permit an agency to take advantage of another agency's experience, expertise, or excess capacity and capability, not merely to avoid legislative restrictions by dumping money or work on another agency.

This condition does not mean the performing agency must have all the required equipment and personnel already on hand before it may properly accept an *Economy Act* order. When necessary, an agency may procure additional supplies or equipment or add additional temporary personnel to perform the work. However, the work or service must be within the scope of activities it normally performs. The *Economy Act* does not provide the performing agency any additional authority it would not otherwise have.[6]

**(4) Lower cost.** The *Economy Act* was never intended to replace normal contracting with the private sector with interagency orders. The fourth condition—the ordering agency must determine that it cannot obtain the goods or services "as conveniently or cheaply" from a private contractor—makes that clear.[7]

Use of the *Economy Act* is permissive, not mandatory. Even if a determination is made that the government cost is lower, the ordering agency may forego the *Economy Act* and contract directly with the private sector. However, the converse is not true. If the agency cannot determine the other agency can provide what is needed as conveniently or cheaply, the use of the Economy Act is improper.[8]

Although doing so is not required by the law, GAO regards documenting the determinations found in (2) and (4) (interest of the government and lower cost) as a sound practice and a desirable internal control.[9] Documentation of these determinations are the first thing auditors look for when reviewing interagency transactions, so it is important to maintain such documentation for all *Economy Act* orders.

## 241. What happens if, in the course of satisfying an *Economy Act* order, the performing activity acquires property or a capital asset to perform the work? Who owns the property or capital asset?

If the ordering agency paid for the entire asset through an advance of funds to the performing agency, the asset belongs to the ordering agency for its use or disposal. However, if the ordering agency pays upon completion of the order, and the performing agency acquires property with its own funds, the property belongs to the performing agency and only the depreciation of the asset that occurred during the work period should be charged to the ordering agency.[10]

Agencies must be careful about acquiring substantial amounts of equipment to satisfy customer orders if it could be concluded they were not originally "in a position" to perform the needed work. Property acquired should be incidental to the performance of the work.

## 242. Are there any other requirements for *Economy Act* transactions?

The recording statute and case law in the form of GAO decisions require that *Economy Act* transactions be evidenced by a written order or agreement in advance, signed by the responsible administrative officer of each of the departments or offices concerned. The written agreement normally establishes a ceiling on the ordering agency's financial obligation and also establishes the scope of the undertaking and the rights and obligations of the parties.[11]

GAO recommends that the agreement contain at least all of the following:[12]

- Legal authority for the agreement
- Terms and conditions of performance
- The cost of performance, including appropriate ceilings when cost is based on estimates
- Mode of payment (advance or reimbursement)

- Any applicable special requirements or procedures for assuring compliance
- Approvals by authorized officials.

## 243. Who is covered by the *Economy Act*?

The Act covers all three branches of government. It applies to virtually all federal organizations, including government corporations, temporary boards, and commissions.[13] The common element of applicability is that the entity must be an agency or instrumentality of the United States government. Therefore, the Act does not apply to the District of Columbia government or to the National Guard, except when the Guard is called into federal service.[14]

A few other exceptions to its coverage are Indian tribes, agencies of the United Nations, American Samoa, and presidential inaugural committees. Because of language in the *Postal Reorganization Act*, the *Economy Act* does not apply to the Postal Service. It also does not apply to nonappropriated fund instrumentalities.[15]

It is important to remember the *Economy Act* is for federal-to-federal transactions, not transactions with state or local governments.

Transactions within an agency are authorized under the *Economy Act*. Thus, two bureaus or offices within the same department or agency may engage in *Economy Act* dealings, but they must be funded under separate appropriations. GAO has also opined that the Economy Act does not apply to separate appropriations of a single bureau or office.[16]

## 244. How are the payments to be made for reimbursable work performed under an *Economy Act* agreement?

The payment provision of the *Economy Act* is 31 U.S.C. 1535(b):

> Payment shall be made promptly by check on the written request of the agency or unit filling the order. Payment may be in advance or on providing the goods or services ordered and shall be for any part of the estimated or actual cost as determined by the agency or unit filling the order. A bill

> submitted or a request for payment is not subject to audit or certification in advance of payment. Proper adjustment of amounts paid in advance shall be made as agreed to by the heads of the agencies or units on the basis of the actual cost of goods or services provided.[17]

Key provisions in this paragraph include:

- There are two types of payments—advance and reimbursement.
- The performing agency decides how payment is to be made.
- Payment may be made as a lump sum or in installments.
- Audit and certification prior to payment is not required.
- Payments made in advance are adjusted up or down when the actual cost is known.

## 245. How are the proceeds that are reimbursed to be credited to the accounting records?

Payments are credited to the appropriation or fund against which charges were made to fill the order. This means crediting the payments to both the correct appropriation and the correct fiscal year. Thus, a reimbursement is credited to the fiscal year in which it was earned, that is, the fiscal year actually charged by the performing agency, without regard to when the reimbursement is actually made. Therefore, if reimbursement is made after the performing activity's appropriation has expired, the reimbursement must be credited to the expired account. If the appropriation has already closed, the reimbursement goes to miscellaneous receipts.[18]

## 246. Receiving reimbursement late in the fiscal year or, worse yet, after the funds have expired creates big problems for the performing activity. What can we do to make sure we don't lose the funds?

The performing activity's choices are:

- Require advance payment.

- Bill the ordering agency promptly as soon as the work is completed.
- Bill periodically as portions of the work are done.

## 247. Are there any exceptions to the rule that reimbursements must be credited to the expired appropriation?

A major exception applies to the Department of Defense. Under authority found in Title 10, the DoD may, at its option, credit *Economy Act* reimbursements to the expired appropriation that earned the reimbursement or to the appropriation current at the time of collection.[19]

## 248. The *Economy Act* authorizes the reimbursement of "actual cost." What is included in the term *actual cost*?

Unfortunately, the law provides no precise definition of *actual cost*. A starting point in the discussion is the notion of augmentation. Agencies must avoid unauthorized augmentation of their appropriations. Charging too much would augment the appropriation of the performing agency; charging too little would augment the appropriation of the ordering agency. In other words, get what you pay for, and pay for what you get.[20] (However, the Department of Defense has a statutory exception, 10 U.S.C. 2571(b), that allows one military department or organization, at its discretion, to provide supplies or services to another military entity on a nonreimbursable basis—that is, free.)

Let's start with the easy part, direct costs. These are the easily identifiable costs associated with providing the goods or services. The two major direct costs are direct labor and direct materials or equipment.

In addition, some indirect costs that can be proportionately attributed to the transaction are part of actual costs that may be charged. Examples include supervision and rent paid to the General Services Administration attributable to space used in the course of performing *Economy Act* work.[21]

Depreciation is normally not recoverable because it is not funded out of currently available appropriations.[22] Also not recoverable are pure general and administrative costs, such as human resources support to the performing unit, or perimeter security, which would be incurred regardless of whether the unit was performing work for the customer.

The *Economy Act* does not require precision in the actual cost determination. So long as a reasonable method of allocation of costs is used, the *Economy Act* is satisfied.[23] Agencies must avoid overcharging a particular customer with "deep pockets" because that would effectively subsidize other customers or would result in an augmentation of the performing agency. Either outcome is improper.

## 249. What happens if the ordering agency cancels the order prior to completion of the work, but the performing activity has incurred some costs?

Just as with a contract with the private sector, if the government terminates for convenience, the performing agency should not have to bear the loss for expenses already incurred.[24] Thus, despite the fact that no goods or services have actually been provided, the performing agency may bill for such actual costs incurred, and the ordering agency is required to pay.

## 250. Does issuing an *Economy Act* order constitute an obligation on the part of the ordering agency?

The customer's funds are obligated upon acceptance of the order by the performing agency. The previous chapter talked about what constitutes an obligation and when it occurs. *Economy Act* orders are governed by 31 U.S.C. 1501(a)(1), which states an obligation is recordable upon evidence of a binding agreement.[25] The "binding agreement" requirement is met by acceptance of the order by the performing agency.

## 251. Are *Economy Act* orders subject to the *bona fide* needs rule?

Absolutely. In fact, soon after the passage of the original *Economy Act*, some agencies tried to use the Act to extend the obligational life of their appropriation by ignoring the *bona fide* needs rule. To counter this practice, Congress enacted another provision that created the so-called "deobligation" provision of the *Economy Act*.[26]

## 252. What does the "deobligation" provision of the *Economy Act* say?

31 U.S.C. 1535(d) states:[27]

> An order placed or agreement made under this section obligates an appropriation of the ordering agency or unit. The amount obligated is deobligated to the extent that the agency or unit filling the order has not incurred obligations, *before the end of the period of availability of the appropriation*, in –
>
> (1) providing goods or services; or
>
> (2) making an authorized contract with another person to provide the requested goods or services.

The second sentence of the paragraph above lays out the requirement that the performing agency must incur obligations to fill the order within the period of availability of the appropriation being used. Otherwise, the funds must be deobligated. As previously mentioned, the purpose was to prevent the *Economy Act* from being used as a subterfuge to continue the availability of appropriations beyond the period provided in the appropriations act.

To restate the requirement, funds obligated under the *Economy Act* must be deobligated at the end of their period of availability (fiscal year or multiple-year period) to the extent the performing agency has not performed the work or has not itself incurred valid obligations as part of its performance.[28]

If the performing agency is using in-house resources to accomplish the work, it must finish the work before the ordering agency funds expire. Anything not finished is deobligated. Alternatively, if the performing agency is using a contract to get the work done on behalf of the ordering agency, the contract must be awarded prior to expiration of the customer funds.

The deobligation requirement applies to both advance payments and payments made by way of reimbursement.[29]

## 253. So the nature of the obligation is different under an *Economy Act* order than it is with a contract with a commercial vendor?

Exactly. Suppose an agency wants a study conducted on the state of the morale of its workforce. It could enter into a contract with a commercial vendor just days before the end of the fiscal year, knowing that most of the work would be done in the following year. Assuming the need was legitimate, the obligated funds would remain available to pay for the entire job, despite the fact the funds expired early in the performance period by the contractor.

But if the same requirement is undertaken with another federal agency under the Economy Act, only the work actually performed prior to September 30 could be paid for from the original appropriation. Any remaining work would require a new *Economy Act* order citing the new fiscal year funds.

## 254. Aren't there other statutory authorities besides the *Economy Act* that might be used to authorize an interagency transaction?

There are many of them, and this is an important point: When reimbursable work is done under the authority of any of the other statutory authorities, *the deobligation requirement does not apply.*[30] Only the *Economy Act* has this particular deobligation quirk. Reimbursable work performed under other authorities follows the same rules as obligations with commercial firms.

Thus, it is advantageous to cite something other than the *Economy Act* as the authority for the interagency transaction. Generally speaking, such statutory authority belongs to the performing activity, not to the ordering activity. It is the performing activity that must have some other statutory authority to use its appropriations to support others, to be able to bill for the costs, and to apply the reimbursement against its appropriation.

## 255. What are the ground rules for using other statutory authorities (so-called non-*Economy Act*) as a basis for reimbursable work?

First, follow any specific provision of the specific authority. For example, the statute might authorize the agency to do reimbursable work for state or local governments, or even the private sector, and be reimbursed for it.

Beyond the specifics in the non-*Economy Act* statute, it is generally accepted that the rules used for *Economy Act* agreements are a good place to start when implementing non-*Economy Act* agreements. For example, the "funds are available" requirement of the *Economy Act* would apply to all non-*Economy Act* authorities as well. The major exception is the deobligation requirement: The ordering agency is *not* required to deobligate its funds for work not yet accomplished under non-*Economy Act* authority.

## 256. What are some examples of other statutory authorities that grant agencies the right to perform reimbursable work for other?

There are many. Here is a list of several:[31]

- *Government Employees Training Act* – 5 U.S.C. 4104
- Tennessee Valley Authority – 16 U.S.C. 831h-1
- District of Columbia – 31 U.S.C. 1537
- National Academy of Sciences – 36 U.S.C. 150303
- Inspection of Personal Property – 40 U.S.C. 504
- National Archives and Records Administration – 44 U.S.C. 2116(c)
- Consumer Product Safety Commission – 15 U.S.C. 2076(g).

## 257. It is surprising that interagency work doesn't have to be audited or certified prior to payment. Why is that the case?

A payment to another federal agency differs from a payment to a private party in that an erroneous payment to another agency does not result in an actual loss of funds to the United States. If an erroneous payment between departments is made, it is easily corrected upon discovery through an account adjustment.[32] Because of the reduced risk of loss of funds, audit and certification of these payments is not required.

## 258. In an interagency transaction, who is ultimately responsible for the proper use of the customer's funds—the customer or the performing activity?

The customer—the ordering activity—remains accountable for the proper use of its funds.[33] Clearly, the performing activity should not knowingly accept an order that will violate purpose, time, or amount, but the onus is on the funds holder (the customer) to properly execute its funds.

## 259. When personnel are detailed or loaned from one agency to another, does the *Economy Act* apply?

It does. Details of personnel are a common type of *Economy Act* transaction. Further, absent specific statutory authority to the contrary, details of personnel between agencies or between separately funded components of the same agency may not be done on a nonreimbursable basis. This is because a nonreimbursed detail would create an augmentation of the receiving agency's appropriation as well as violate the purpose law on the part of the lender of the personnel.[34]

Brief periods of time and small numbers of personnel, where the cost involved is minimal, are allowed under GAO's *de minimis* exception. (GAO has not defined the limits of *de minimis*, but certainly one person detailed for two hours would be fine. Twenty people detailed for one day would not.)

## 260. May an agency loan property to another agency without seeking reimbursement?

Yes, so long as no other costs are incurred in loaning the property. However, the *Economy Act* should not be used for loans for indefinite periods because that amounts to a permanent transfer in disguise.

Permanent transfers of property are authorized under the *Economy Act*, but payment is required.[35]

## 261. What are some restrictions on the type of work that can be performed under the authority of the *Economy Act*?

One restriction is the rule that the *Economy Act* may not be used for services that the performing agency is required by law to provide and for services for which it receives appropriations. This rule is required to prevent agencies from agreeing to reallocate funds between themselves in circumvention of the appropriations process.[36] For example, if a GAO audit enables an agency to recover overcharges, the amounts recovered may not be paid to GAO to help defray the cost of conducting the audit. Conducting audits is GAO's job, and it receives an appropriation to conduct them. Reimbursing GAO for conducting an audit would amount to an augmentation of its appropriation.

Further, if a service is required to be provided on a nonreimbursable basis, the fact that the providing agency's appropriation is inadequate does not permit reimbursement by the receiving agency.[37] Lack of funds is not an excuse to do an end-run around the law.

If a particular service is authorized but not required, some circumstances would allow reimbursement. For example, the Secret Service is statutorily required to provide protective services to specified officials. Other officials, not on the protected list, may obtain such protective services from the Secret Service on an *Economy Act* reimbursable basis.[38]

## 262. What are the advantages of using an *Economy Act* order if the performing agency is merely issuing a contract? Why doesn't the ordering activity just issue the contract itself?

When the *Economy Act* was first passed, it did not allow for contracting out a requirement to satisfy a customer requirement. Congress gave that authority to five agencies in 1942, and then in 1982 it amended the *Economy Act* to authorize all agencies to obtain goods and services by contract in fulfilling *Economy Act* orders. The legislative history of the 1982 Act describes three potential advantages:[39]

1. An agency having only an occasional requirement in a specific area could turn to an agency with substantial experience in the area for assistance. This would eliminate the need to duplicate the requisite expertise.
2. The Act creates the potential for wider use by the government of quantity discounts or other benefits of large purchases.
3. The Act permits an agency to use another agency that has some, though not all, of the capability to do the required work by allowing the performing agency to simply contract out the part of the work that it cannot do.

## 263. How did granting that authority (to obtain goods and services by contract in fulfilling *Economy Act* orders) in 1982 work out?

In the late 1980s and early 1990s, there were reported abuses under the *Economy Act.* The Senate Committee on Governmental Affairs coined a new term, *off-loading,* in its report, *Off-Loading: the Abuse of Inter-Agency Contracting to Avoid Competition and Oversight Requirement.*

Among the abuses the report cited were the use of off-loading to avoid competition, to direct contracts to favored contractors, to improperly obligate expiring year-end appropriations, and to make a variety of inappropriate purchases.[40]

Congress responded in 1993 and 1994 with two pieces of legislation, one for military procurements and the other for civilian procurements. They are virtually identical and require the following:

- Off-loading is permitted only if the performing agency (1) has an existing contract for the same or similar goods or services, (2) is better qualified to enter into or administer the contract by reason of capabilities or expertise the ordering agency does not have, or (3) is specifically authorized by law to act in that capacity.

- Off-loads must be approved in advance by an authorized official of the ordering agency.
- The payment of any fee in excess of the performing agency's actual costs or, if not known, estimated costs is prohibited.[41]

## REVOLVING FUNDS

### 264. What are revolving funds, and how do they differ from the reimbursable transactions discussed previously in this chapter?

In its simplest form, a revolving fund is nothing more than a special kind of Treasury account. Most Treasury accounts are either receipt accounts or expenditure accounts. You can put money into a receipt account, but you can't take money out. You can take money out of an expenditure account, but you can't put any into it. They are one-way accounts.

Revolving funds have an account that goes both ways: You may deposit funds into it and then disburse from it on a continuing basis. Thus, the funds revolve through the account. They are established by acts of Congress to finance an entity or activity that will operate on a business-like basis. The technical definition is "a fund established by Congress to finance a cycle of businesslike operations through amounts received by the fund."[42] The legislation that authorizes a revolving fund is a permanent, indefinite appropriation.[43] The legislation serves as the revolving fund's charter and normally prescribes the purpose of the fund and limits on how it may operate.

The revolving fund's continuing availability is what distinguishes the fund from a reimbursable appropriation.[44] In the case of a reimbursable appropriation, the reimbursements are available only during the same period that the appropriation itself is available, whereas in a revolving fund, monies are paid in and out over and over again for the same purpose.

## 265. It is my understanding that revolving funds are no-year funds. Does that mean that if I advance my fiscal year appropriation to a revolving fund, those dollars suddenly become no-year funds?

Although it is true that revolving funds are, in fact, no-year funds, customer funds provided to a revolving fund retain their fiscal limitations until the revolving fund has earned them, at which time the money is recognized as revenue to be credited to the revolving fund.[45] So the revolving fund has to do the work to earn the revenue, at which time the revenue becomes no-year funds.

## 266. What are the advantages of a revolving fund?

Proponents cite several advantages:[46]

- Just one appropriation for the entire operation, hence a simpler funding structure
- Clearer picture of an activity's profit or loss
- Less budget distortion because expenditures are reflected on a net basis
- Increased flexibility because the agency does not have to continually ask Congress for money
- Provides agencies the authority to enter into interagency agreements independent of the *Economy Act*—and therefore not subject to the deobligation requirement of the *Economy Act.*

## 267. May an agency administratively establish a revolving fund?

No. An agency would need explicit and specific statutory authority.[47] The reason is that revolving funds are, in essence, exceptions to the miscellaneous receipts statute, which states that money received must be deposited in Treasury unless otherwise provided in law. Because this requirement is statutory, any exceptions to it must also be statutory.

## 268. Once a revolving fund receives a charter from Congress, where does it get the money to get started?

Normally the legislation that sets up the fund provides, through direct appropriation or some other means of financing an initial infusion of working capital (called the fund's *corpus*) so it can cover startup costs and finance operations until its operational receipts start coming in.[48] From then on, the revolving fund operates in a manner similar to a private business, providing goods or services to customers on an ongoing basis and charging the customer prices that will cover the fund's full cost of operation. The long-term goal of the vast majority of revolving funds is to break even.

## 269. After receiving the initial cash *corpus*, do revolving funds ever get additional money from Congress?

That is always an option. If a fund is failing to meet its goal of breaking even, or if there has been a significant impairment of capital (for example, a building has burned down), Congress may enact additional appropriations.

## 270. Is there more than one kind of revolving fund?

There are three broad categories of revolving funds—public enterprise, trust, and intragovernmental. They all share the common attributes of a revolving fund: (1) They are created by act of Congress; (2) they operate as combined receipt and expenditure accounts; and (3) they authorize use of the receipts without further congressional action.[49]

- *Public enterprise revolving funds*—These funds derive most of their receipts from sources outside the federal government. Normally they sell something to the public.[50] Examples are the Postal Service, the Southwestern Power Administration, and the United States Mint Public Enterprise Fund.

- *Trust revolving funds*—These funds typically collect money from taxes or contributions, hold them in trust, and disburse them to qualified recipients.[51] Examples are the Civil Service Retirement Trust Fund, Social Security Trust Fund, and Employees' Life Insurance Fund.

- *Intragovernmental revolving funds*—These funds' receipts come primarily from other government agencies, programs, or activities. They are designed to carry out a cycle of business-like operations with other federal agencies or separately funded components of the same agency. There are subcategories, which include stock funds, industrial funds, supply funds, working capital funds, and franchise funds.[52] Examples include United States Geological Survey Working Capital Fund, Air Force Working Capital Fund, and Department of Veterans Affairs Franchise Fund.

## 271. Since revolving funds aren't dependent on direct appropriations from Congress, does that mean that all the appropriations law rules we've been discussing don't apply to revolving funds? I've heard that revolving funds are just a big pot of cash that can be used for most any purpose without worrying about appropriations rules.

That is a misconception shared by many people. A revolving fund is an appropriation—a permanent, indefinite appropriation. Therefore, funds in a revolving fund are appropriated funds.[53] It follows, then, that funds in a revolving fund are subject to the same purpose, time, and amount limitations and restrictions applicable to all other appropriated funds.

As to the myth of being able to use revolving funds for any purpose, remember that each revolving fund was established by statute. The chartering statute states the purpose of the fund and what the funds may be used for. While direct appropriations find their purpose statements in the annual appropriations acts, the purpose statements of revolving funds are in their charters.[54] If the charter is silent on a given object, the "necessary expense" doctrine is applied the same as with any other appropriation.

As mentioned in a previous chapter, revolving funds are subject to all the provisions of the *Antideficiency Act*—the same as direct appropriations.

## 272. If revolving funds are no-year funds, would the time rules, including *bona fide* needs, apply?

Receipts and collections earned through the fund's operations are available without further congressional action and without fiscal year limitation. Thus, the time availability of revolving fund balances is comparable to that of no-year appropriations, which are available until expended. The same time rules apply, including the absence of the need to apply the *bona fide* needs rule.[55]

Remember, however, that if the money of the revolving fund's customer is from a fixed-term appropriation, the customer must satisfy the various time rules applicable to its own appropriation, including the *bona fide* needs rule. Thus, it is improper for a customer agency using a fiscal-year appropriation to place an order with a revolving fund at the end of the fiscal year without a legitimate need in an attempt to use the revolving fund to extend the life of the appropriation.

## 273. Are revolving funds exempt from the prohibition against augmentation?

They are not exempt. Although a revolving fund is an exception to the miscellaneous receipts statute, it is not a blanket exception. The exception goes only so far as the governing legislation specifies. The legislation establishing a revolving fund prescribes what may go into the fund. Depositing anything not expressly authorized by the statute is an improper augmentation. Note that refunds, such as recovery of erroneous payments, as discussed in a previous chapter, may be deposited even though not specified in the governing legislation.

Examples of unauthorized augmentation are:[56]

- Transferring funds to the revolving fund from other appropriation accounts without statutory authority or in excess of statutory authority

- Retaining a funded reserve for accrued annual leave after the employees have transferred to another agency
- Retaining jury service fees remitted by an employee paid from a revolving fund.

## USER FEES

### 274. Most of the discussion in this chapter has focused on intragovernmental transactions. What authority does an agency have—or need—to provide goods or services to the private sector, and collect and retain the proceeds?

There are three parts to this issue.

First, an agency may not use its appropriation to produce or supply materials or services to private parties without specific statutory authority.[57] So before the question of charging or retaining user fees even comes up, the agency must have the legal authority to provide anything to nonfederal entities.

Second, when Congress authorizes an agency to provide goods or services to the public, it decides how to finance that activity. One possibility is subsidization, which means funding it from appropriated funds, spreading the cost among all taxpayers. The other possibility is user financing, through the imposition of a user fee. A *user fee* is defined as "a price charged by a governmental agency for a service or product whose distribution it controls" or "any charge collected from recipients of Government goods, services, or other benefits not shared by the public."[58] Examples are the cost of a postage stamp or the fee to obtain a passport. Agencies must have specific statutory authority to charge a user fee.

Third, assuming it is given the authority to charge a user fee, may the agency retain it? This answer is controlled by the miscellaneous receipts statute. The agency would need a specific statutory exception to the miscellaneous receipts statute to retain the fees in its accounts.[59]

To summarize, for an agency to keep money it receives from the public, it must have statutory authority for all three of the following:

1. Providing goods or services to the public
2. Charging a user fee
3. Retaining the user fee.

## NOTES

1. U.S. Government Accountability Office, *Principles*, Chap. 12, 12-22.
2. Ibid., 12-24.
3. Ibid., 12-25.
4. Ibid., 12-26.
5. Ibid., 12-27.
6. Ibid.
7. Ibid., 12-29.
8. Ibid.
9. Ibid.
10. Ibid., 12-28.
11. Ibid., 12-30.
12. Ibid.
13. Ibid., 12-31.
14. Ibid., 12-32.
15. Ibid.
16. Ibid., 12-33.
17. Ibid.
18. Ibid., 12-35.
19. Ibid., 12-36.
20. Ibid., 12-38.
21. Ibid., 12-40.
22. Ibid.
23. Ibid., 12-42.
24. Ibid.
25. Ibid., 12-44.

26. Ibid., 12-45.
27. Ibid., 12-43.
28. Ibid., 12-45.
29. Ibid.
30. Ibid., 12-46.
31. Ibid., 12-80–12-85.
32. Ibid., 12-50.
33. Ibid., 12-53.
34. Ibid., 12-56.
35. Ibid., 12-61.
36. Ibid., 12-68.
37. Ibid., 12-69.
38. Ibid., 12-70.
39. Ibid., 12-73.
40. Ibid., 12-75.
41. Ibid., 12-76.
42. Ibid., 12-86.
43. Ibid., 12-87.
44. Ibid., 12-88.
45. Ibid.
46. Ibid.
47. Ibid., 12-89.
48. Ibid., 12-92.
49. Ibid., 12-97.
50. Ibid.
51. Ibid., 12-98.
52. Ibid.
53. Ibid., 12-106.
54. Ibid., 12-109.
55. Ibid., 12-114.
56. Ibid., 12-126.
57. Ibid., 12-141.
58. Ibid., 12-143.
59. Ibid., 12-182.

# Chapter 7
# Continuing Resolutions

It has become increasingly common that Congress does not enact appropriations bills before October 1 of each year. To avoid government shutdowns caused by a "funding gap," Congress uses continuing resolutions to keep the government running. This chapter describes continuing resolutions and the rules and restrictions that go with them.

## 275. What is meant by the term *continuing resolution*?

GAO defines it as follows:[1]

> An appropriation act that provides budget authority for federal agencies, specific activities, or both to continue in operation when Congress and the President have not completed action on the regular appropriation acts by the beginning of the fiscal year.

Thus, continuing resolutions are temporary appropriations acts intended to be stop-gap measures enacted to keep existing federal programs functioning after the expiration of previous budget authority and until regular appropriations are enacted.

## 276. Are continuing resolutions a recent phenomenon?

They have been around for well over 100 years. At one time they were called *temporary resolutions*. In the early 1960s the term *continuing resolution* came into widespread use.[2]

They are also extremely common. In 31 of the fiscal years between 1977 and 2011, action was not completed on a majority of the appropriations bills by the start of the fiscal year. In ten of those years, none of the bills were finished by October 1. Fiscal year 2001 set a record with 21 continuing resolutions.[3]

## 277. Are all continuing resolutions the same?

Although they take different forms from time to time, the following example from 2005 is typical of most:

> Such amounts as may be necessary under the authority and conditions provided in the applicable appropriations act for fiscal year 2004 for continuing projects or activities including the costs of direct loans and loan guarantees (not otherwise specifically provided for in this joint resolution) which were conducted in fiscal year 2004, at a rate for operations not exceeding the current rate, and for which appropriations, funds, or other authority was made available in the following appropriations Acts . . . .[4]

The resolutions also include language that authorizes spending until regular appropriations are enacted or the expiration date of the resolution is reached, whichever occurs first.

## 278. How much may an agency spend under a continuing resolution?

Unlike regular appropriations, continuing resolutions do not typically include a specified sum of budget authority. They are indefinite appropriations—"such amounts as may be necessary."[5] Therefore, it is up to each agency to determine its spending authority under the continuing resolution, in accordance with the language it contains.

Most continuing resolutions direct agencies to operate at the lowest of:[6]

- House-passed amount
- Senate-passed amount
- Agency budget estimate
- "Current rate."

The current rate is most often the lowest of these amounts, so it becomes the controlling factor.

## 279. What does the term *current rate* mean?

The current rate is equivalent to the total amount of money that was available for obligation for an activity during the fiscal year immediately preceding the one for which the continuing resolution is enacted.[7] It refers to a sum of money, not a program level. Thus, if costs for a program go up, that means the program will be able to provide results at a reduced level. In simple terms, it doesn't include a factor for inflation.

If funding in the preceding year covered only a part of that year, the agency may annualize the previous year's appropriation to determine the current rate.[8] Thus, if a program was funded in the prior year on April 1 through a supplemental appropriation at a level of $10 million, this year's current rate for that program would be $20 million, assuming a requirement to operate the program for the entire fiscal year.

For programs funded by multiple-year appropriations, the current rate must be reduced by any unobligated, and still available, balances carried over into the present year.[9] This is to prevent the program's being funded at a higher level in the present year than it was in the preceding year.

## 280. If a continuing resolution is for a three-month period, does that mean I may obligate only one-fourth of my last year's amount?

Absent congressional language directing otherwise, an agency may determine the pattern of its obligations under a continuing resolution so long as it operates under a plan that will keep it within the rate-for-operations limit set by the resolution.[10] If an agency normally obligates a high percentage of its annual budget in the first quarter of the fiscal year, it may continue that pattern under the resolution. Prior-year obligation rates, while informative, are not absolutely controlling. If the agency can demonstrate a need for a different spending pattern, it may spend at that rate, so long as it has a spending plan to remain within the limits of the resolution on an annual basis.

## 281. Do agencies receive an apportionment of budget authority under continuing resolutions?

The apportionment requirement applies to continuing resolutions, just as it does to regular appropriations.[11]

OMB normally issues an OMB Bulletin on apportionment requirements each year. Typically, OMB allows for an automatic apportionment of the "daily rate."[12] That is, if your current rate is $365 million, or $1 million per day, and the continuing resolution is for 30 days, you would automatically be apportioned $30 million and would be authorized to obligate that amount without seeking a specific apportionment. However, if the agency needs more than $30 million, it would have to seek an apportionment from OMB for a larger amount before obligating in excess of its automatic apportionment.

## 282. What happens if an agency is operating under continuing resolutions deep into the fiscal year, and then Congress cuts its budget below the prior-year levels?

If Congress appropriates a total that is less than obligations already incurred, the obligations remain valid and are charged to the continuing resolution.[13] In such circumstances, however, agencies are expected to make their best effort to remain within the amount of the final appropriation.

## 283. We hear that "no new starts" are allowed under continuing resolutions. What does that mean?

For many years, continuing resolutions often contained a section stating that no funds made available under the resolution "shall be available to initiate or resume any project or activity" that was not conducted during the preceding fiscal year.[14] That means if you didn't perform the project or activity last year, you can't do it this year under the continuing resolution.

However, in more recent years Congress has softened the language somewhat. Rather than limiting funds to programs that were actually conducted in the prior year, more recent resolutions prohibit the use of funds for "any project or activity for which appropriations, funds, or other authority were not available" during the preceding year.[15] Thus, if an agency had the authority and funds to carry out a particular program in the preceding year, even if the agency didn't "start" it, that program is not a new project or activity in the current year. So the question to ask is this: "Could the agency have started the program last year?" If the answer is "yes," the program is not a new start in the current fiscal year.

## NOTES

1. U.S. Government Accountability Office, *Principles,* Chap. 8, 8-2.
2. Ibid.
3. Ibid., 8-3.
4. Ibid., 8-4.
5. Ibid., 8-6.
6. Ibid.
7. Ibid., 8-11.
8. Ibid.
9. Ibid., 8-13.
10. Ibid., 8-15.
11. Ibid., 8-18.
12. Ibid.
13. Ibid., 8-19.
14. Ibid., 8-24.
15. Ibid.

# Chapter 8
# Accountability and Liability of Individuals

The idea that a person entrusted with money is accountable for it is a common notion. If a cashier in a retail store comes up short at the end of the day, it's likely the cashier will have to make up the shortage from personal funds. The government does not operate any differently.

This chapter examines the accountability, liability, and relief from liability of government employees who are involved in the handling of funds or who have specific responsibilities in the payment process. Such people are called accountable officers.

## 284. What is an accountable officer?

Accountable officers include such officials as certifying officers, disbursing officers, and other employees who by virtue of their employment have custody of government funds.[1]

It is important to note that GAO has ruled that accountable officer status and liability may be imposed only through statute.[2] An agency does not have the authority to confer accountable officer status to anyone not so designated in statute.

## 285. Who is included among accountable officers?

Certifying officers do not hold public funds in their custody; they are responsible for certifying vouchers for payment. They are responsible for the legality of proposed payments and are liable for the amount of illegal or improper payments that result from their certification.[3]

Disbursing officers are employees who are designated to disburse moneys and render accounts in accordance with laws and regulations governing the disbursement of public funds.[4] The Treasury Department has disbursing officers who disburse funds for most civilian agencies. DoD has disbursing officers who do the same for that Department.

DoD is unique in that it has a third class of individuals who are accountable for errors they make. They are called Departmental accountable officials, and were created in 2002 when a statute authorized DoD to appoint employees engaged in developing, verifying, approving, and processing payments.[5] These employees provide source information, data, or service to a certifying or disbursing officer in support of the payment process. They are pecuniarily liable for erroneous payments resulting from negligence in performing these duties.

## 286. My agency has people in the Budget Office who certify funds availability prior to obligation. Are they considered certifying officers?

No. Many government employees make official "certifications" of one type or another. Managers certify time and attendance reports. Contracting or program officials might certify that goods or services have been received and accepted on behalf of the government. Those sorts of duties do not make them certifying officers for the purposes of accountability and liability. For the purposes of this discussion, we are referring only to those appointed officials who certify vouchers for payment to be made by disbursing officers. Certifying officers must be designated in writing.

## 287. For how much is a certifying or disbursing officer liable?

An accountable officer is liable for the amount of any physical loss or improper payment, less any amount recovered.[6] If the proper amount of a payment was $5000 but the certifying officer certified the voucher and payment was made for $7000, the liability is $2000. Collection efforts would attempt to recover the overpayment, and any amount received from the payee would reduce the amount of the liability.

## 288. Does the government need to prove that the accountable officer is liable?

No. Whenever there is a physical loss of funds or an improper payment made, the responsible accountable officer is instantly liable for the entire amount of the loss.[7] The accountable officer is automatically assumed to have been negligent. The onus is on the accountable officer to demonstrate that he or she was not negligent when requesting relief.

## 289. How does relief differ from liability?

It is important to distinguish between liability and relief. It is not the denial of relief that makes an accountable officer liable. As noted previously, the basic legal liability of an accountable officer arises automatically by virtue of the loss. It is not affected by any lack of fault or negligence on the officer's part.

Relief is a separate process. Lack of fault may be taken into consideration in the decision to grant or deny relief from the liability.[8]

## 290. Suppose an accountable officer makes an erroneous payment based on direction from a senior official in the agency. Wouldn't that move the liability to the senior official and insulate the accountable officer?

No—unless the senior official had been appointed as an accountable officer as well. Accountability and liability are reserved for properly appointed accountable officers.[9] The agency would be able to take administrative disciplinary action against the senior official for authorizing or directing an improper payment, but it could not impose pecuniary liability.

## 291. Doesn't that put disbursing officers and certifying officers in an awkward, precarious position?

It often does. Accountable officers must resist pressure to take actions they do not believe to be proper. They do have one fallback position: Accountable officers have the statutory authority to request an advance decision from GAO prior to certifying or disbursing a payment they find questionable. So long as accountable officers follow the GAO decision, they are insulated from liability for that transaction.[10]

## 292. What sorts of government funds are included in the category of accountable public funds?

The scope is very broad. Accountable public funds include appropriated funds, funds received by the government from nongovernmental sources, and funds held in trust.[11] These would include imprest funds, flash rolls, travel advances, receipts, and items that are the equivalent of cash. This last category includes food stamps, Government Transportation Requests, military payment certificates, traveler's checks, and treasury bonds with interest coupons attached.

## 293. Who grants relief from liability?

The answer depends on the agency involved, the amount involved, and whether the loss was a physical loss or an erroneous payment. Figure 8-1 summarizes the various possibilities.

| Agency | Situation | Amount | Who Grants Relief? |
|---|---|---|---|
| Civilian (non-DOD) | Physical Loss | $3000 or less | Agency |
| | | Over $3000 | GAO |
| | Erroneous Payment | $100 or less | Agency |
| | | Over $100 | GAO |
| DOD Armed Forces * | Physical Loss | Any Amount | DOD (DFAS) |
| | Erroneous Payment | | |
| DOD Civilian Agencies | Physical Loss | $3000 or less | DOD (DFAS) |
| | | Over $3000 | GAO **/DOD(DFAS) *** |
| | Erroneous Payment | $100 or less | DOD (DFAS) |
| | | Over $100 | GAO **/DOD (DFAS) *** |

**Figure 8-1: Relief of Liability**

* For the Coast Guard, a non-DOD Armed Force, the Secretary of Homeland Security grants relief in all instances.

** Per GAO opinion (B-307693, 4/12/2007). GAO states that GAO has relief authority over Defense Agencies.

*** Per DOD Regulation (DOD 7000.14R). DOD Regulation states that DOD (DFAS) has relief authority over all DOD activities.

Note that GAO and DoD have a difference of opinion about who holds relief-granting authority for the DoD civilian agencies that are not part of the armed forces (Army, Navy, Marine Corps, and Air Force). A 2007 decision by GAO maintains that GAO has such authority. However, the DoD Financial Management Regulation (relevant portions updated in 2009) shows that the Defense Finance and Accounting Service, by means of delegation from DoD, grants or denies relief for the entire department.

## 294. I notice in the Relief of Liability chart that physical loss and erroneous payment are treated separately. Are there different standards for granting relief for the two types of losses?

Indeed there are. Let's talk about physical loss of funds first.

Remember from earlier discussion that the presence or absence of negligence has nothing to do with an accountable officer's liability. The officer is liable for all losses but may be relieved from that liability if found to be free from fault or negligence. The standard of negligence that GAO uses is that of simple or ordinary negligence, not gross negligence.[12] The standard has been stated as what a reasonably prudent and careful person would have done to take care of his or her own property of like description under like circumstances.[13]

This is an objective standard; that is, it does not vary with such factors as the age or experience of the particular accountable officer. Likewise, inadequate training or supervision does not affect the standard. Further, the doctrine of comparative negligence (allocating the loss based on the degree of fault) does not apply under the relief statutes.[14] It is an all or nothing proposition—relief is either granted or denied. There is no such thing as partial relief.

The accountable officer who suffers a loss is presumed negligent and has the burden of proof to show a lack of negligence. If the facts indicate that negligence was the proximate cause of the loss, relief will be denied.[15]

There are cases, however, when relief is granted even if the accountable officer was negligent. This would occur if it can be shown that the negligence was not the "proximate cause" of the loss.[16] If the accountable officer can show that some other factor was the proximate cause of the loss, relief may be granted even if the officer was, in fact, negligent.

A good illustration of the proximate cause situation occurred when 12 men in minibuses broke into the American Embassy in Lagos, Nigeria.[17] They broke into the cashier's office and were carrying the safe down the stairs when they dropped it. The safe popped open, and the burglars fled with the money that had been inside. The safe had opened because the cashier had not locked it—clearly an act of negligence. However, even if the safe had been locked, the burglars had demonstrated they could carry away the safe. Had it not come open, they would have loaded it into a minibus and opened it elsewhere. Thus, the cashier's failure to lock the safe, though negligent, was not the proximate cause of the loss.

Another way to garner relief is to argue that "pervasive laxity" in the protection and administration of funds was the cause of the loss.[18] If agency policies or practices put funds at risk, and the accountable officer has no control over those policies, one can argue that relief should be granted under the concept of pervasive laxity. For example, suppose agency regulations call for safe combinations to be changed annually. However, despite requests by the cashier using a safe to change the combination, it hasn't been changed in three years and the previous cashiers still have the combination to the safe. Relief would be granted if an unexplained loss occurred. Poor agency security does not guarantee relief, however. One factor considered is the accountable officer's efforts to improve the situation.

Other circumstances where relief would normally be granted include fire or natural disaster[19] and loss by theft (when there is clear evidence that a theft took place and no evidence the accountable officer was implicated).[20]

On the other hand, decisions have found the following factors to be not relevant, and insufficient to rebut the presumption of negligence:[21]

- Extra duties by the accountable officer
- Shortage of personnel

- Financial hardship of repaying the loss
- Good work record; long period of loyal and dependable service
- Heavy workload
- Inexperience
- Inadequate training
- Inadequate supervision.

## 295. What are the standards of relief for erroneous payments?

Certifying officers must certify the legality and correctness of each payment that passes through their hands on the way to the disbursing officer. When all payments were processed manually, the certifying officer would review the supporting documentation for each payment voucher and sign each voucher individually. The increased use of automated payment systems has changed the way certifying officers must operate.[22]

While recognizing that the certifying officer's basic legal liability remains, GAO opined that the conditions in which a certifying officer may be relieved under an automated payment system must be different to reflect the new realities.[23]

To apply these new standards, the evidence that payments are accurate must relate to the system rather than to individual transactions. Certifying and disbursing officers must be provided with information that the system they are relying on is functioning properly. In addition, reviews must be done at least annually to determine that automated systems are operating effectively and can be relied on to produce payments that are accurate and legal.[24]

Thus, when considering requests for relief, the basic question is the reasonableness of the certifying officer's reliance on the system to continually produce legal and accurate payments.[25]

Statistical sampling may be used for vouchers up to $2500. A certifying or disbursing officer acting in good faith and in conformity with an authorized statistical sampling procedure will not be held liable for any certification or payment on a voucher that was not subject to specific examination because of the procedure.[26]

Although relying on statistical sampling will enable a certifying officer to avoid liability on payments not sampled, there is still the question of the standards of relief for other erroneous payments.

There are two standards of relief:[27]

1. The certification was based on official records and the certifying officer did not know, and by reasonable diligence and inquiry could not have discovered, the actual facts.
2. The obligation was incurred in good faith, the payment was not specifically prohibited by statute, and the United States received value for the payment.

Under either standard, relief may be denied if the agency fails to diligently pursue collection action against the recipient of the improper payment.

Relief may be requested by the agency on behalf of the certifying/disbursing officer or directly by the certifying/disbursing officer. Relief requests must present sufficient information to permit GAO to make a proper determination.[28]

## 296. If GAO denies relief, is that the end of the matter? Or may the agency or accountable officer appeal?

When GAO has denied relief, the agency or the accountable officer (through appropriate administrative channels) may ask GAO to reconsider. GAO will not hesitate to reverse a decision shown to be wrong. Denials of relief are often based not on the merits of the case, but simply on the failure of the original request to include sufficient information to enable an independent evaluation.[29]

## 297. If relief is denied, how is the money collected from the accountable officer?

If the loss cannot be recovered from the improper recipient and relief has been denied to the accountable officer, the accountable officer becomes indebted to the government for the amount involved. It is the agency's responsibility to initiate collection action in accordance with the *Federal Claims Collection Act and Standards.*[30] If the accountable officer is still employed by the government, his or her pay will be withheld until the funds are repaid. Reasonable installments are authorized, and the agency determines the amount of the installment payments. For employees no longer on the payroll, collection from retirement funds is also authorized. Accountable officers still on the payroll may have their retirement accounts "flagged" should they terminate employment before satisfying the debt.[31]

## NOTES

1. U.S. Government Accountability Office, *Principles,* Chap. 9, 9-11.
2. Ibid., 9-11.
3. Ibid., 9-13.
4. Ibid., 9-14.
5. Ibid., 9-12.
6. Ibid., 9-31.
7. Ibid., 9-10.
8. Ibid.
9. Ibid., 9-7.
10. Ibid., 9-93.
11. Ibid., 9-20.
12. Ibid., 9-45.
13. Ibid.
14. Ibid., 9-46.
15. Ibid., 9-48.
16. Ibid., 9-51.
17. Ibid., 9-52.
18. Ibid., 9-70.

19. Ibid., 9-60.
20. Ibid., 9-61.
21. Ibid., 9-74.
22. Ibid., 9-78.
23. Ibid., 9-79.
24. Ibid.
25. Ibid., 9-80.
26. Ibid., 9-81.
27. Ibid., 9-95.
28. Ibid., 9-96.
29. Ibid., 9-135.
30. Ibid., 9-139.
31. Ibid., 9-140.

# Chapter 9
# Grants and Agreements

The federal government provides assistance to state and local governments and private nonprofit organizations. This assistance comes in many forms, all of which are designed to support some element of national policy. Grants and cooperative agreements constitute the vast majority of government assistance programs. They are the subject of this chapter.

## 298. What is a grant?

The *Intergovernmental Cooperation Act* defines a grant as "money, or property provided instead of money, that is paid or provided by the United States government under a fixed annual or total authorization, to an eligible beneficiary." The Act defines eligible beneficiaries as including state and local governments as well as certain private nonprofit organizations. Specifically excluded from the definition are loans, shared revenue, and payments under a research and development procurement contract.[1] GAO's budget glossary (see Appendix 2) defines a grant as a "federal assistance award making payment in cash or in kind for a specific purpose." GAO goes on to say that the term *grant* is used broadly and may include nongovernmental recipients in addition to state or local governments, while the term *grant-in-aid* normally refers to a grant to a state or local government.[2]

Thus, a federal grant is a legally authorized transfer of money, property, or services to another party (the grantee) for a purpose or activity the government has chosen to assist.

## 299. What is a cooperative agreement, and how does it differ from a grant?

Cooperative agreements are very much like grants in that they transfer something of value to a recipient to accomplish a public purpose. The key difference from a grant is that under cooperative agreements, the federal agency providing the assistance has more direct involvement with the recipient in carrying out the activity.[3]

## 300. Are the fiscal law rules substantially different for grants and cooperative agreements?

The rules for grants and cooperative agreements are nearly the same. However, there are considerable differences between the rules for these assistance programs and the rules for procurement contracts. Because much of this book has focused on the use of funds for contractual relationships, the following discussion on grants and cooperative agreements will highlight how assistance programs differ from contracts.

## 301. Does that mean that a grant or cooperative agreement is not a contract between the government and the grantee?

Not exactly. Grants are viewed by the courts as a type of contract. They contain all the elements of a contract—competent parties, proper subject matter, consideration, and a meeting of the minds. However, the contract analogy has its limits.[4]

For example, take the issue of consideration. A grant is a form of assistance to a designated class of recipients to meet recognized needs. These needs, by definition, are not needs for goods or services required by the federal government itself. The needs are those of the nonfederal entity that Congress has decided to assist in the public interest.[5] An illustration would be if the government awards a grant that provides 50 percent of the cost of a new building, with the grantee to pay the other 50 percent. At a later time, if funds are available, the government is free to modify the grant and increase the government's share to 75 percent or even 100 percent. The government receives no additional consideration by increasing its share. Such a transaction would not be allowable under a procurement contract, while it is commonplace with grants.

## 302. Are there other differences between assistance programs and contracts?

There are several. Under contract law, ambiguities in contract language are decided against the government as the drafting party. That is not the case with grants.[6]

Contract law has a doctrine of "impossibility of performance," which states that contract terms may not impose a condition that is physically impossible to perform. The impossibility of performance doctrine does not apply to grants.[7]

Additionally, *quantum meruit* expenditures to a grantee are not authorized because the government does not receive tangible benefit in the traditional contract sense. The "contract implied in fact" concept also does not apply to grants because a grant is a sovereign act binding the government only to the extent of its express undertakings.[8]

## 303. Can you summarize the similarities and difference between assistance programs and contracts?

Grants are a hybrid, with both similarities to and differences from contracts. They can be viewed as contracts with statutory and regulatory terms superimposed upon them.[9] Thus, the rights and obligations of the parties cannot be determined solely by looking at the terms of the grant agreement itself. The applicable grant statute, its legislative history, the grantor agency's regulations, and OMB guidance must all be considered.

However, the awarding of a grant does create certain legal obligations. If a grantee does what it has committed itself to do and incurs allowable costs, the government is obligated to pay those costs. Conversely, the government has a right to expect that the grantee will use the grant funds only for authorized grant purposes, in accordance with the terms and conditions of the grant. The grantor agency has the right to oversee the expenditure of funds by the grantee to ensure the money is used only for authorized purposes, and it is the duty of the grantee to account to the grantor for its use of the funds.[10]

## 304. Is there an "umbrella" statute that prescribes how assistance programs are to operate?

Congress enacted the *Federal Grant and Cooperative Agreements Act* in 1977. It contains criteria for when grants and cooperative agreements are to be used and how they are to be administered.[11]

## 305. How does an agency decide whether to use a procurement contract, grant, or cooperative agreement?

The *Federal Grant and Cooperative Agreements Act* established the following standards:[12]

- *Procurement contracts*—An agency is to use a procurement contract when the principal purpose of the instrument is to acquire (by purchase, lease, or barter) property or services for the direct benefit or use of the United States government.
- *Grant agreements*—An agency is to use a grant agreement when the principal purpose of the relationship is to transfer a thing of value (money, property, services) to the recipient to carry out a public purpose of support or stimulation authorized by a law of the United States instead of acquiring property or services for the direct benefit of the government, and substantial involvement *is not* expected between the agency and the recipient when carrying out the activity.
- *Cooperative agreements*—An agency is to use a cooperative agreement when the principal purpose of the relationship is to transfer a thing of value (money, property, services) to the recipient to carry out a public purpose of support or stimulation authorized by a law of the United States instead of acquiring property or services for the direct benefit of the government, and substantial involvement *is* expected between the agency and the recipient when carrying out the activity.

## 306. What are examples where "substantial involvement is expected"?

The following might require substantial federal involvement in the performance of the activity (as opposed to an oversight role that is inherent in all grant agreements as well as cooperative agreements).[13]

- Novel or complex undertakings, e.g., some construction, information systems development, and demonstration projects
- Collaborative research, planning, or problem solving
- Interrelationships among projects in areas such as applied research
- Early stages of ongoing programs where standards are being developed or during a period of adjustment until recipient capability has been developed.

## 307. Apart from the previously mentioned differences between assistance programs and contracts, what are the similarities in the application of basic fiscal law principles to grants and cooperative agreements?

The fundamental principles of appropriations law apply to grants just as they do to any other expenditure. Among the principles that apply to grants are:[14]

- Congress decides what, when, and how much to authorize, and also may impose conditions and restrictions to the use of grant funds (congressional power of the purse).
- Grant purposes and conditions must be constitutional.
- Grant conditions imposed by federal statute are binding and prevail over any inconsistent state law.
- The purpose law (31 U.S.C. 1301(a)) applies to assistance agreements. Grant funds may be obligated and expended only for authorized grant purposes.

- Funds must be obligated by the grantor agency within their period of availability. Obligation generally occurs at the time of the award of the grant.
- The *bona fide* needs rule applies to grants and cooperative agreements. However, the principle of severability does not apply to these assistance programs. Thus, the agency must have a *bona fide* need to award a grant and do so during the agency funds' period of availability. But the award of the grant satisfies the requirement. The grantee need not perform during the period of availability, and the period of time the grantee has to use the funds is not limited (although the grant statute or the grantor agency may impose time limits on a grantee's use of funds).
- Grant obligations and expenditures are subject to the *Antideficiency Act*. Agencies may not award grants and incur obligations in advance or in excess of the amount available.
- A federal agency is not eligible to receive grant funds from another agency because that would improperly augment the appropriations of the receiving agency.
- Agency regulations issued in accordance with grant authorizing legislation carry the force and effect of law.
- Grantees are not agents of the United States government, and therefore the government has no liability associated with a contract between a grantee and a third party.
- The United States is not liable for torts committed by its grantees.

## 308. What are some of the differences in how fiscal law rules are applied to assistance agreements?

Grant funds in the hands of a grantee largely lose their character and identity as federal funds. GAO stated:[15]

> It consistently has been held with reference to Federal grant funds that, when such funds are granted to and accepted by the grantee, the expenditure of such funds by the grantee for the purposes and objects for which made is not subject

> to the various restrictions and limitations imposed by Federal statute or our decisions with respect to the expenditure, by Federal departments and establishments, of appropriated moneys in the absence of a condition of the grant specifically providing to the contrary.

Therefore, except as provided by the grant statute, regulation, or the grant agreement, the expenditure of grant funds by a state government is subject to the laws of that state, rather than federal laws applicable to direct expenditures by federal agencies.

Thus, many of the statutes governing the use of funds by federal agencies do not apply once the grant money is in the hands of the grantee. Among the restrictions that do not apply are:[16]

- Dual compensation restriction for federal employees is not applicable to grantee employees.
- Restrictions on payments to retired military officers.
- Immunity from payment of state and local taxes. Because the grantee is not a federal agent, it is not immune from property and sales taxes.
- Adequacy of appropriations act, which prohibits entering into contracts for amounts in excess of appropriations for that purpose.
- Prohibition against purchasing aircraft without specific statutory authority.
- Prohibition against paying a nonfederal person's travel expenses to a meeting.
- Requirement for specific authority to establish a revolving fund.
- General prohibition against advance payments. However, if the federal government advances grant funds to a state or other entity, any interest earned on the advanced funds belongs to the federal government, not the grantee.

## 309. Suppose a grantee uses the grant funds for the intended purpose but in the process earns some income (not interest on advances) through the operation of its program, for example, through sales, fees, etc. May the grantee keep those funds?

Except in the case of the sale of real property paid for by the grant, the grantee may retain this sort of program income unless the grant legislation or the grant itself dictates otherwise.[17]

## 310. If a grantee is unable to perform and the grant agreement is terminated, may the agency issue a replacement grant using the same fiscal year funds even if those funds have expired?

The rule and the conditions are the same as for replacement contracts.[18] If the agency funds have expired at the time a replacement grant is to be issued, those same funds may be used for the replacement grant if:

- There is a continuing *bona fide* need for the grant project.
- The replacement grant is for the same purpose and scope.

The replacement grant should be awarded within a reasonable time period.

## 311. Suppose a grantee is advanced the grant funds and uses them for an unauthorized purpose. Is the grantee indebted to the government for that amount?

If no allowable costs of an equal amount are subsequently incurred, the grantee is required to return the amount of the improper charge to the government. The agency may not waive this requirement to repay.[19]

## NOTES

1. U.S. Government Accountability Office, *Principles*, Chap. 10, 10-3.
2. Ibid., 10-4.

3. Ibid., 10-5.
4. Ibid., 10-9.
5. Ibid.
6. Ibid., 10-10.
7. Ibid.
8. Ibid.
9. Ibid., 10-11.
10. Ibid., 10-12.
11. Ibid., 10-13.
12. Ibid., 10-14.
13. Ibid., 10-15.
14. Ibid., 10-28–10-58.
15. Ibid., 10-69.
16. Ibid., 10-70–10-77.
17. Ibid., 10-89.
18. Ibid., 10-107.
19. Ibid., 10-115.

# Chapter 10
# Nonappropriated Fund Instrumentalities

The previous chapter described the nature of grants and cooperative agreements and explained how fiscal law rules did or did not apply to such assistance programs. Likewise, this chapter focuses on nonappropriated funds instrumentalities—what they are and how the rules that govern their operations are similar to, or different from, those for appropriated funds.

## 312. What is the definition of *nonappropriated fund instrumentality* (NAFI)?

Unfortunately, there is no precise definition of what is, or is not, a nonappropriated fund activity. Although activities recognized as NAFIs share certain traits, not all NAFIs are created equal. Therefore, beyond a few basic similarities, one must look at the origin, source of funding, and legal authorities of each NAFI to determine which laws apply to it.

The one underlying basis for all NAFIs is that nonappropriated funds include those funds that are *not* derived from an annual appropriations act or a law enacting a permanent, indefinite appropriation. Therefore, these funds are generally not subject to the same fiscal controls as appropriations.[1]

Broadly speaking, there are two types of NAFIs—morale, welfare, and recreational (MWR) entities and all other NAFIs. The MWR entities are associated with the armed forces and share a long, common history. These armed forces NAFIs were created to meet the MWR needs of the military members and their dependents. On the other hand, there is little commonality among the non-armed forces NAFIs.[2]

## 313. What are some examples of NAFIs?

Armed forces NAFIs include base and post exchanges, enlisted and officer clubs, bowling centers, golf courses, and movie theaters.

Non-armed forces NAFIs exist within agencies on a case-by-case basis. These NAFIs are created by statute, which normally defines any fiscal limitations. Two examples are the Board of Governors of the Federal Reserve and the Raisin Administrative Committee of the Department of Agriculture. These entities do not serve MWR needs of government employees. On the other hand, NASA has a NAFI, the Exchange Council, which does provide MWR benefits to NASA employees.

## 314. Are NAFIs government entities or not?

NAFIs are considered government entities. However, they are not federal agencies or government corporations. Nor are they typical private or commercial enterprises. They are a hybrid—a combination of government and private activity. A common trait is that NAFIs operate mainly with funds generated from their own activities.[3]

NAFIs enjoy certain benefits of being government entities. One is an exemption from locally imposed taxes levied directly on the NAFI. Just as the federal government is immune from such direct taxation, so are NAFIs. However, Congress may consent to state taxation of its instrumentalities, as it does for the collection of state taxes on gasoline sold through post exchanges on military installations when the fuel is not for use by the United States.[4]

Another benefit is immunity from suit. As instrumentalities of the United States, sovereign immunity applies, and the government may be sued only when it consents to be sued. Again, Congress may (and has for certain claims) waive sovereign immunity for NAFIs.[5]

## 315. Are NAFI employees considered employees of the United States?

They are not considered employees of federal agencies or employees of the United States government unless a statute specifically states otherwise.[6] They are not covered by the *Civil Service Reform Act*, the *Civil Service Retirement Act*, or the *Whistleblower Protection Act*.

## 316. May an agency send an Economy Act order to a NAFI for goods or services?

The *Economy Act* does not apply to NAFIs. Obtaining goods or services from a NAFI is tantamount to obtaining them from non-governmental, commercial sources.[7]

## 317. May a NAFI compete for government work just like a contractor?

Yes. NAFIs may compete to provide goods or services to agencies in the competitive procurement process.[8]

## 318. What are the rules for spending nonappropriated funds?

There is no one answer. The use of nonappropriated funds is governed by statute and agency regulation over the individual NAFI. It is important to remember that many, if not most, NAFIs are for morale, welfare, and recreation purposes. Generally speaking, appropriated funds are not available for MWR activities and therefore nonappropriated funds are often used in cases where appropriated funds can't be used.

NAFIs may spend nonappropriated funds without regard to the purpose, time, and amount restrictions discussed at length in this book. They are bound only by statutory language and agency regulation in administering these funds.

## NOTES

1. U.S. Government Accountability Office, *Principles,* Chap. 15, 15-233.
2. Ibid., 15-233.
3. Ibid., 15-235.
4. Ibid., 15-262.
5. Ibid.
6. Ibid., 15-266.
7. Ibid., 15-250.
8. Ibid., 15-251.

# Appendix 1

# Can Your Agency Use Appropriated Funds for Meals and Light Refreshments?

In general, an agency may not use appropriated funds to purchase items considered personal expenses, such as food, without specific authority. B-301184, Jan. 15, 2004.

The decision tree below identifies the statutory authority and limited exceptions that may permit an agency to provide food to employees at their duty stations:

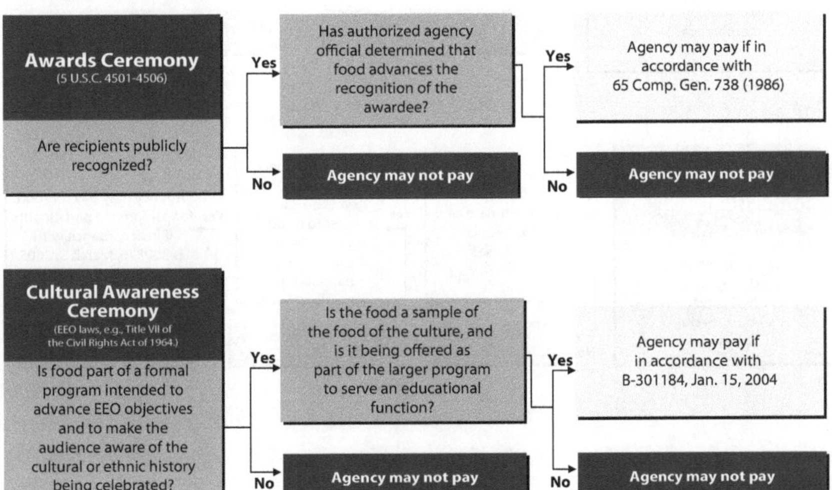

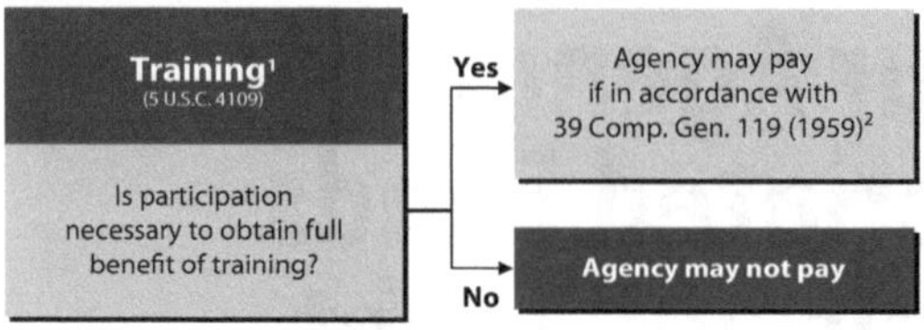


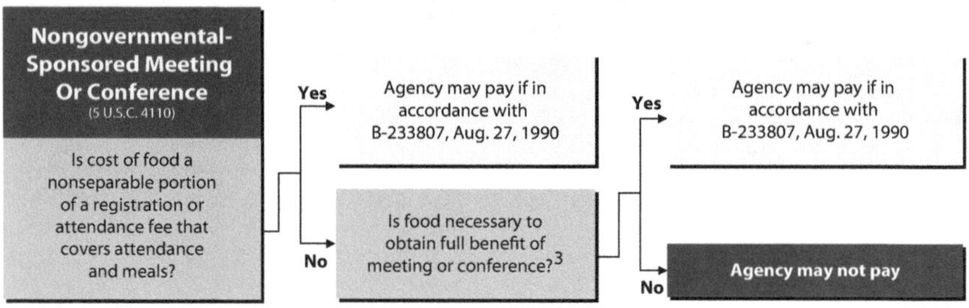


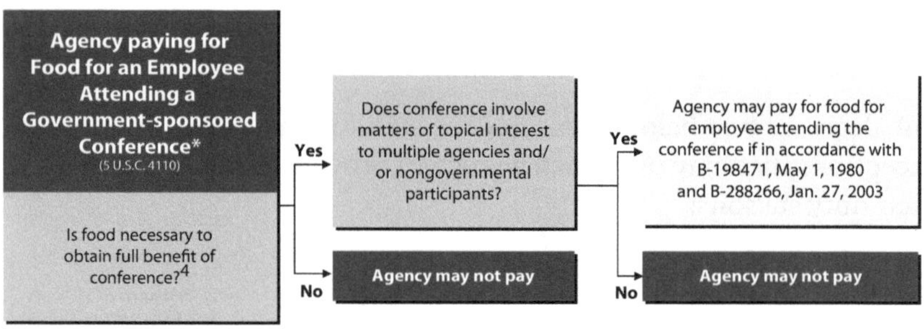


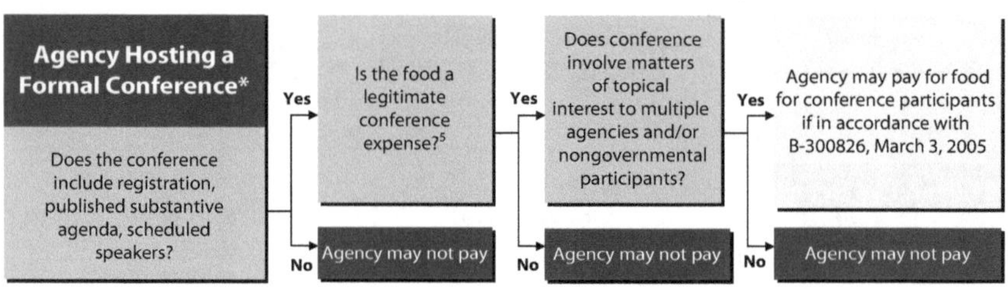


* Without statutory authority to charge a fee and retain the proceeds, the host agency may not charge a registration or other fee to defray the costs of providing food.

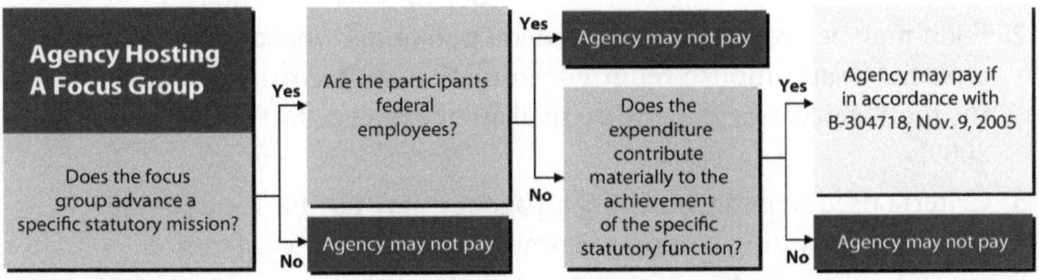


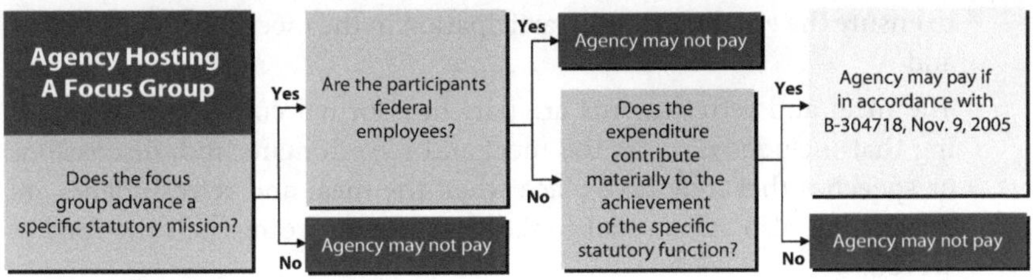


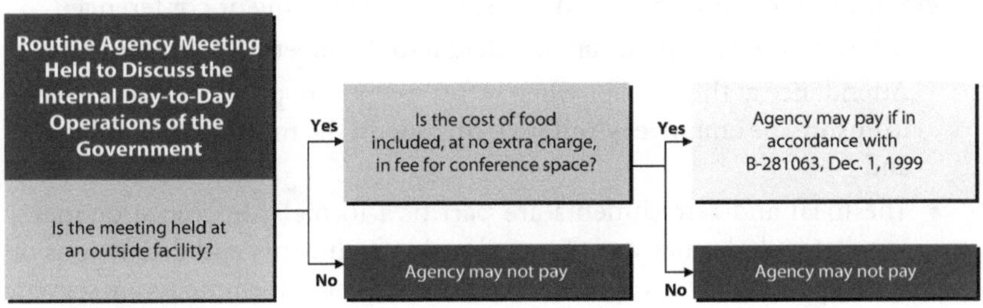


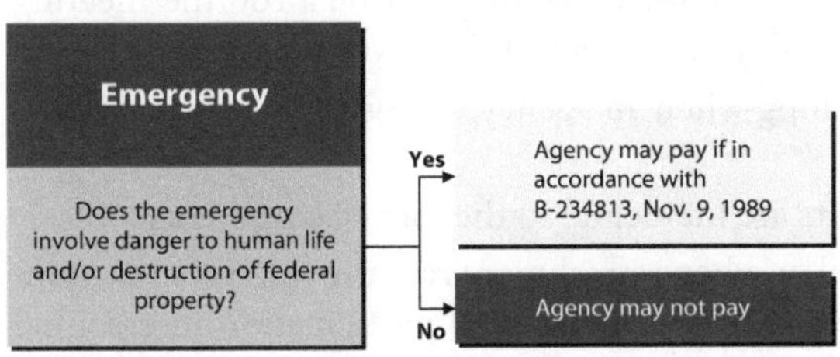


## NOTES

1. All training must comply with the Government Employees Training Act definition of training in 5 U.S.C. 4101(4).

2. Food may be provided to non-federal personnel whose participation is essential to accomplish required simulation antiterrorism training and the food is necessary to ensure realism of exercise. B-317423, March 9, 2009.
3. Criteria used in determining if an agency may pay for food for an employee attending a nongovernmental meeting or conference:
   - Meals and refreshments are incidental to the meeting or conference,
   - Attendance at the meal or when refreshments are provided is important to ensure the employees' full participation in the meeting or conference, and
   - The meal and refreshments are part of a formal conference or meeting that includes not just the meal and refreshments and, discussions or speeches that may take place when the meal and refreshments are served, but also substantial functions separate from when the food is served.
4. Criteria used in determining if an agency may pay for food for an employee attending a government-sponsored meeting or conference:
   - Meals and refreshments are incidental to the meeting or conference,
   - Attendance at the meal or when refreshments are provided is important to ensure the employees' full participation in the meeting or conference, and
   - The meal and refreshments are part of a formal conference or meeting that includes not just the meal and refreshments and discussions or speeches that may take place when the meal and refreshments are served, but also substantial functions separate from when the food is served.
   - In addition, the meeting or conference may not be a routine meeting that involves the day-to-day operations of the government.
5. Criteria used in determining when an agency, as host, may pay for food at a formal conference:
   - Meals and refreshments are incidental to the formal conference,
   - Attendance at the meal or when refreshments are provided is important for the host agency to ensure attendees' full participation in essential discussions and speeches concerning the purpose of the formal conference, and
   - The meal and refreshments are part of a formal conference that includes not just the meal and refreshments and discussions or speeches that may take place when the meal and refreshments are served, but also substantial functions separate from when the food is served.

# Appendix 2
# Glossary of Terms

## ACCOUNT

A separate financial reporting unit for budget, management, or accounting purposes. All budgetary transactions are recorded in accounts, but not all accounts are budgetary in nature. Some accounts do not directly affect the budget; they are used purely for accounting purposes.

Budget accounts are used to record all transfers within the budget, whereas other accounts (such as a deposit fund, credit financing, and foreign currency accounts) are used for accounting purposes for funds that are nonbudgetary in nature.

The Office of Management and Budget (OMB), in consultation with the Department of the Treasury, assigns account identification codes reflecting appropriations enacted in appropriations laws. Treasury establishes and maintains a system of accounts that provides the basic structure for the U.S. Government Standard General Ledger Chart of Accounts.

### *Appropriation Account*

The basic unit of an appropriation, generally reflecting each unnumbered paragraph in an appropriations act. An appropriation account typically encompasses a number of activities or projects and may be subject to restrictions or conditions applicable to only the account, the appropriations act, titles within an appropriations act, other appropriations acts, or the government as a whole.

### *Account in the President's Budget*

An account used by the federal government to record outlays (expenditure accounts) and income (receipt accounts), primarily for budgeting or management information purposes, but also for accounting purposes. All budget and off-budget accounts are classified as either expenditure or receipt (including offsetting receipt) accounts and by fund group. Budget and off-budget transactions fall within one of two fund groups: federal funds and trust funds.

All federal fund and trust fund accounts are included within the budget (that is, they are on budget), unless they are excluded from the budget by law. Federal and trust funds excluded from the budget by law are classified as off-budget. The term *off-budget* differs from the term *non-budgetary*. Nonbudgetary activities (such as credit financing accounts) do not belong in the budget under existing concepts, while off-budget accounts belong on budget under budget concepts but are excluded from the budget under terms of law.

### Federal Fund Account

Budgetary account composed of monies collected and spent by the federal government, other than those designated as trust funds. Federal fund accounts include general, intragovernmental, public enterprise, and special fund accounts.

#### *General Fund Account*

Account in the U.S. Treasury holding all federal money not allocated by law to any other fund account.

##### General Fund Receipt Account

A receipt account credited with all collections that are not earmarked by law for another account for a specific purpose. These collections are presented in the president's budget as either governmental (budget) receipts or offsetting receipts. They include taxes, customs duties, and miscellaneous receipts.

##### General Fund Expenditure Account

An appropriation account established to record amounts appropriated by law for the general support of federal government activities and the subsequent expenditure of these funds. It includes spending from both annual and permanent appropriations.

### Intragovernmental Fund Account

Expenditure account authorized by law to facilitate financing transactions primarily within and between federal agencies.

#### Intragovernmental Revolving Fund Account

An appropriation account authorized to be credited with collections from other federal agencies' accounts that are earmarked to finance a continuing cycle of business-type operations, including working capital funds, industrial funds, stock funds, and supply funds. According to OMB, collections of intragovernmental revolving fund accounts are derived primarily from within the government. For example, the franchise fund operations within several agencies provide common administrative services to federal agencies on a fee-for-service basis. (*See also* Working Capital Fund.)

#### Management Fund Account

An account established by the Treasury that is authorized by law to credit collections from two or more appropriations to finance activity that does not involve a continuing cycle of business-type operations. Such accounts do not generally own a significant amount of assets, such as supplies, equipment, or loans, nor do they have a specified amount of capital provided (a corpus). The Navy Management Fund is an example of such an account.

##### *Consolidated Working Fund Account*

A subset of management funds. These are special working funds established under the authority of section 601 of the Economy Act (31 USC 1535, 1536) to receive advance payments from other agencies or accounts. Consolidated working fund accounts are not used to finance the work directly, but only to reimburse the appropriation or fund account that will finance the work to be performed.

Monies in consolidated working fund accounts are available for the same amount of time as those in the accounts advancing the funds. Consolidated working fund accounts are shown as separate accounts on Treasury's books but are not separately identified in the president's budget. The transactions of these accounts are included in the presentation of the appropriation or fund account actually performing the service or providing the materials.

#### *Public Enterprise Revolving Fund Account*

A type of revolving fund that conducts cycles of businesslike operations, mainly with the public, in which it charges for the sale of products or services and uses the proceeds to finance its spending, usually without requirement for annual appropriations. Most government corporations are financed by public enterprise funds. (*See* Revolving Fund.)

#### *Special Fund Account*

Federal fund account earmarked by law for a specific purpose.

#### Special Fund Receipt Account

A receipt account credited with collections that are earmarked by law but included in the federal funds group rather than classified as trust fund collections. These collections are presented in the president's budget as either governmental (budget) receipts or offsetting receipts. (*See also* Earmarking.)

#### Special Fund Expenditure Account

An appropriation account established to record appropriations, obligations, and outlays financed by the proceeds of special fund receipts. (*See also* Earmarking.)

#### Trust Fund Account

Account designated as a trust fund by law, regardless of any other meaning of the term *trust fund.* A trust fund account is usually a receipt, an expenditure, or a revolving fund account. Except in rare circumstances (for example, Indian trust funds), a trust fund account imposes no fiduciary responsibility on the federal government. For a fuller discussion of trust funds, see *Federal Trust and Other Earmarked Funds: Answers to Frequently Asked Questions* (GAO-01-199SP). (*See also* Earmarking.)

#### *Trust Fund Expenditure Account*

An appropriation account established to record appropriated amounts of trust fund receipts used to finance specific purposes or programs under a trust agreement or statute.

### Trust Revolving Fund Account

A trust fund expenditure account that is an appropriation account authorized to be credited with collections and used, without further appropriations action, to carry out a cycle of business-type operations in accordance with statute.

### *Trust Fund Receipt Account*

A receipt account credited with collections classified as trust fund collections. These collections are recorded as either governmental receipts or offsetting receipts.

## *Accounts For Purposes Other Than Budget Presentation*

### Clearing Account

An account that temporarily holds general, special, or trust fund federal government collections or disbursements pending clearance to the applicable receipt or expenditure accounts.

### Deposit Fund Account

A nonbudgetary account established to account for collections that are either held temporarily and later refunded or paid upon administrative or legal determination as to the proper disposition thereof, or held by the government, which acts as banker or agent for others. Deposit fund accounts are paid out at the direction of the depositor.

Examples include savings accounts for military personnel, state and local income taxes withheld from federal employees' salaries, and payroll deductions for the purchase of savings bonds by civilian employees of the government.

Deposit fund balances are accounted for as liabilities of the federal government. These accounts are not included in the budget totals because the amounts are not owned by the government. Therefore, the budget records transactions between deposit funds and budgetary accounts as transactions with the public. Deposit fund balances may be held as invested or uninvested balances. However, because the Treasury uses the cash in the accounts to satisfy the government's immediate cash requirements, to the extent that they are not invested in federal debt, changes in uninvested deposit fund balances are shown as a means of financing the deficit in the budget.

### Foreign Currency Fund Account

An account established by the Treasury for foreign currency that is acquired without payment of U.S. dollars. Examples of such accounts are those setup through the Agricultural Trade Development and Assistance Act (7 USC 1691–1736g).

### Suspense Account

A combined receipt and expenditure account established to temporarily hold funds that are later refunded or paid into another government fund when an administrative or final determination about the proper disposition is made.

### Transfer Appropriation (Allocation) Accounts

Accounts established to receive and disburse allocations. Such allocations and transfers are not adjustments to budget authority or balances of budget authority. Rather, the transactions and any adjustments therein are treated as nonexpenditure transfers at the time the allocations are made. The accounts carry symbols that identify the original appropriation from which monies have been advanced. Transfer appropriation accounts are symbolized by adding the receiving agency's department prefix to the original appropriation or fund account symbol. In some cases, a bureau suffix is added to show that the transfer is being made to a particular bureau within the receiving department. For budget purposes, transactions in the transfer accounts are reported with the transactions in the parent accounts. For further information, see the Treasury Financial Manual. (*See also* Allocation; Nonexpenditure Transfer under Transfer.)

## ADMINISTRATIVE DIVISION OR SUBDIVISION OF FUNDS

Any apportionment or other distribution of an appropriation or fund made pursuant to the Antideficiency Act (31 USC 1511–1519). The appropriation may be divided or subdivided administratively within the limits of the apportionment (31 USC 1513(d)). The expenditure or obligation of the divided or subdivided appropriation or fund may not exceed the apportionment (31 USC 1517(a)). (*See also* Antideficiency Act; Antideficiency Act Violation; Apportionment; Limitation.)

## ADVANCE PAYMENT

An amount paid before the later receipt of goods, services, or other assets. Advances are ordinarily made only to payees to whom an agency has an obligation, and they do not exceed the amount of the obligation.

## ADVANCE APPROPRIATION

Budget authority provided in an appropriations act that becomes available one or more fiscal years after the fiscal year for which the appropriations act was enacted. For example, a fiscal year 2012 appropriations act could provide that the budget authority for a specified activity would not become available until October 1, 2012 (the start of fiscal year 2013) or later. The amount is not included in the budget totals of the year for which the appropriations act is enacted but rather in those for the fiscal year in which the amount will become available for obligation. In the example above, the budget authority would be recorded in fiscal year 2013.

## AGENCY

No one definition of this term has general, government-wide applicability. *Agency* and related terms, such as *executive agency* or *federal agency*, are defined in different ways in different laws and regulations. For example, the provisions of the Budget and Accounting Act of 1921 related to the preparation of the president's budget specifically include the District of Columbia government in the definition of *agency* but exclude the legislative branch or the Supreme Court (31 USC 1101).

## AGENCY MISSION

Term used in section 1105(a)(22) of Title 31 of the *U.S. Code*, which outlines content requirements for the president's budget submission to Congress. Section 1105 requires that the president's budget contain a statement of agency budget authority in terms of agency missions, but this section offers no definition of the term. *Agency mission* generally refers to the purpose of the agency's programs and its component organizations.

In OMB's budget functional classification system, agency missions are distinguished from national needs. *National needs* are generally defined as major functions, while agency missions are usually subfunctions.

## ALLOCATION

For the purposes of budgeting, an allocation is a delegation of an agency's authority, authorized in law, to obligate budget authority and outlay funds to another agency. (The appropriation or fund from which the allocation is made is generally referred to as the *parent appropriation* or *parent fund.*)

An allocation is made when one or more agencies share the administration of a program for which appropriations are made to only one of the agencies or to the president. When an allocation is made, the Treasury establishes a subsidiary account called a *transfer appropriation account*, and the agency receiving the allocation may obligate funds up to the amount included in the account. The budget does not show the transfer appropriation account separately.

Transactions involving allocation accounts appear in the object classification schedule, with the corresponding program and financing schedule, in the president's budget. For more about the treatment of object classification with allocation accounts, see OMB Circular A-11.

For purposes of section 302(a) of the Congressional Budget and Impoundment Control Act of 1974 (2 USC 633(a)), an allocation is the distribution of spending authority and outlays to relevant committees based on the levels contained in a concurrent resolution on the budget.

For purposes of section 302(b) of the Congressional Budget and Impoundment Control Act of 1974 (2 USC 633(b)), an allocation is the distribution of spending authority and outlays to relevant subcommittees based on the levels contained in the concurrent resolution on the budget.

For funds control purposes, an allocation is a further subdivision of an apportionment.

## ALLOTMENT

An authorization given by either an agency head or another authorized employee to his or her subordinates to incur obligations within specified limits. Each agency makes allotments pursuant to specific procedures it establishes in accordance with the general apportionment requirements stated in OMB Circular A-11. The amount allotted by an agency may not exceed the amount apportioned by OMB.

An allotment is part of an agency system of administrative control of funds. The purpose of the system is to keep obligations and expenditures from exceeding apportionments and allotments. (*See also* Administrative Division or Subdivision of Funds; Apportionment; Reapportionment.)

## ALLOWANCE

An amount included in the president's budget request or included in a projection in a congressional resolution on the budget to cover possible additional proposals, such as contingencies for programs whose expenditures are controllable only by statutory change and other requirements.

As used by Congress in concurrent resolutions on the budget, an allowance represents a special functional classification designed to include an amount to cover possible requirements. An allowance remains undistributed until the contingency on which it is based occurs. It is then distributed to the appropriate functional classification.

For agency budgetary accounting and fund control purposes, an allowance is a subdivision of an allotment. For treatment of undistributed allowances, see Function 920 in the table, "Outlays by Function and Sub-function," in the Historical Tables section of the president's budget. (For more details on the government accounting definition of *allowance*, see the U.S. Government Standard General Ledger Chart of Accounts.)

For federal proprietary accounting, an allowance also represents the estimated uncollectible amount of accounts receivable.

## ANTIDEFICIENCY ACT

A federal law that:

- Prohibits the making of expenditures or the incurring of obligations in advance of an appropriation
- Prohibits the incurring of obligations or the making of expenditures in excess of amounts available in appropriation or fund accounts unless specifically authorized by law (31 USC 1341(a))
- Prohibits the acceptance of voluntary or personal services unless authorized by law (31 USC 1342)
- Requires OMB, via delegation from the president, to apportion appropriated funds and other budgetary resources for all executive branch agencies (31 USC 1512)
- Requires a system of administrative controls within each agency (see 31 USC 1514 for the administrative divisions established)
- Prohibits incurring any obligation or making any expenditure in excess of an apportionment or reapportionment or in excess of other subdivisions established pursuant to sections 1513 and 1514 of Title 31 of the *U.S. Code* (31 USC 1517)
- Specifies penalties for deficiencies (*see* Antideficiency Act Violation).

The act permits agencies to reserve funds (that is, withhold them from obligation) under certain circumstances. (*See also* Administrative Division or Subdivision of Funds; Antideficiency Act Violation; Apportionment; Deficiency Apportionment; Deficiency Appropriation; Expenditure; Outlay.)

## ANTIDEFICIENCY ACT VIOLATION

Violation that occurs when one or more of the following happens:

- Overobligation or overexpenditure of an appropriation or fund account (31 USC 1341(a))
- Entering into a contract or making an obligation in advance of an appropriation, unless specifically authorized by law (31 USC 1341(a))

- Acceptance of voluntary service, unless authorized by law (31 USC 1342)
- Overobligation or overexpenditure of an apportionment or reapportionment, or amounts permitted by the administrative control of funds regulations (31 USC 1517(a)).

Once it has been determined that the Antideficiency Act has been violated, the agency head must report to the president and Congress all relevant facts and actions taken and submit a copy of the report to the Comptroller General. Penalties for Antideficiency Act violations include administrative discipline, such as suspension from duty without pay or removal from office. In addition, an officer or employee convicted of willfully and knowingly violating the law shall be fined not more than $5,000, imprisoned for not more than two years, or both (31 USC 1349, 1350, 1518, and 1519). (*See also* Administrative Division or Subdivision of Funds; Antideficiency Act; Expenditure.)

## APPORTIONMENT

The action by which OMB distributes funds available for obligation, including budgetary reserves established pursuant to law, in an appropriation or fund account. Apportionments limit the amount of obligations that may be incurred.

An apportionment divides amounts available for obligation by specific time period (usually quarters), activity, project, object, or a combination thereof. An apportionment may be further subdivided by an agency into allotments, suballotments, and allocations. In apportioning any account, some funds may be reserved to provide for contingencies or to effect savings made possible pursuant to the Antideficiency Act. Funds apportioned to establish a reserve must be proposed for deferral or rescission pursuant to the Impoundment Control Act of 1974 (2 USC 681–688).

The apportionment process is intended to prevent the overobligation of amounts available within an appropriation or fund account, thus avoiding the need for deficiency or supplemental appropriations, and to achieve the most effective and economical use of funds made available for obligation. (*See also* Administrative Division or Subdivision of Funds; Allotment; Antideficiency Act; Deficiency Apportionment; Deficiency Appropriation; Limitation; Reapportionment; Rescission; Supplemental Appropriation.)

## APPROPRIATIONS ACT

A statute, under the jurisdiction of the House and Senate Committees on Appropriations, that generally provides legal authority for federal agencies to incur obligations and to make payments out of the Treasury for specified purposes. An appropriations act fulfills the requirement of article I, section 9, of the U.S. Constitution, which provides that "no money shall be drawn from the Treasury, but in Consequence of Appropriations made by Law." Under the rules of both houses of Congress, an appropriations act should follow the enactment of authorizing legislation. (*See also* Appropriations *under* Forms of Budget Authority *under* Budget Authority; Authorizing Legislation; Limitation.)

The major types of appropriations acts are regular, supplemental, deficiency, and continuing. Regular appropriations acts are all appropriations acts that are not supplemental, deficiency, or continuing. Currently, regular annual appropriations acts that provide funding for the continued operation of federal departments, agencies, and various government activities are considered by Congress annually. From time to time, supplemental appropriations acts are also enacted. When action on regular appropriation bills is not completed before the beginning of the fiscal year, a continuing resolution (often referred to simply as CR) may be enacted in a bill or joint resolution to provide funding for the affected agencies for the full year, up to a specified date, or until their regular appropriations are enacted. A deficiency appropriations act provides budget authority to cover obligations incurred in excess of available budget authority. (*See also* Continuing Appropriation/Continuing Resolution (CR); Supplemental Appropriation; Deficiency Appropriation.)

## AUTHORIZING COMMITTEE

A standing committee of the House or Senate with legislative jurisdiction over the establishment, continuation, and operations of federal programs or agencies. The jurisdiction of such committees extends, in addition to program legislation, to authorization of appropriations legislation. (Normally, authorization of appropriations legislation is a prerequisite for making appropriations for the given programs or agencies.)

An authorizing committee also has jurisdiction in instances in which backdoor authority is provided in the substantive legislation. For further discussion, see the current rules of the House of Representatives and the Senate. (*See also* Authorizing Legislation.)

## AUTHORIZING LEGISLATION

Substantive legislation, proposed by a committee of jurisdiction other than the House or Senate Appropriations Committees, that establishes and continues the operation of a federal program or agency indefinitely or for a specific period or that sanctions a particular type of obligation or expenditure within a program. This term is used in two different ways: to describe legislation enacting new program authority (that is, authorizing the program), and to describe legislation authorizing an appropriation.

Authorization of appropriations legislation authorizes the enactment of appropriations of specific amounts for specific programs and activities to be provided in an appropriations act. An authorization of appropriations is, under congressional rules, a prerequisite for such an appropriation. Thus, for example, a point of order may be raised in either house objecting to an appropriation in an appropriations act that has not been previously authorized by law. An authorization of appropriations may be part of the organic legislation for the agency or program, or it may be separate legislation.

Oftentimes, the authorization of appropriation may be inferred from an appropriation provided in an appropriations act. The authorization of appropriation may specify the amount of budget authority to be included in the appropriations act, or it may authorize the appropriation of "such sums as may be necessary." In some instances, authorizing legislation may contain an appropriation or provide other forms of budget authority, such as contract authority, borrowing authority, or entitlement authority. (*See also* Appropriations Act; Limitation.)

## BUDGET

A detailed statement of anticipated revenues and expenditures during an accounting period. With regard to the federal government, the term *budget* often refers to the president's budget submission to Congress early each calendar year in accordance with the amended Budget and Accounting Act of 1921 and represents proposals for congressional consideration. The president's budget includes requests for budget authority for federal programs and estimates of revenues and outlays for the upcoming fiscal year and, with respect to budget authority requests, in some cases, for future fiscal years. By law, elements of the budget, such as the estimates for the legislative branch and the judiciary, must be included without review by OMB or approval by the president.

In the context of individual federal agencies and their programs, the term *budget* also may be used to refer to their budget submissions or, in response to Congress passing laws providing budget authority, the agencies' plans for spending the funds they were given.

## BUDGET AND ACCOUNTING ACT OF 1921

Legislation that enhanced budgetary efficiency and helped the performance of constitutional checks and balances through the budget process. It required the president to submit a national budget each year and restricted the authority of the agencies to present their own proposals. (See 31 USC 1104, 1105.)

The act gave the president and the newly established Bureau of the Budget (now the Office of Management and Budget) authority for the formulation of the executive branch budget. Congress also took steps to strengthen its oversight of fiscal matters by establishing the General Accounting Office (GAO, renamed the Government Accountability Office in 2004).

## BUDGET AUTHORITY

Authority provided by federal law to enter into financial obligations that will result in immediate or future outlays involving federal government funds. The basic forms of budget authority include appropriations, borrowing authority, contract authority, and the authority to obligate and expend offsetting receipts and collections. Budget authority includes the credit subsidy cost for direct loan and loan guarantee programs, but it does not include the underlying authority to insure or guarantee the repayment of indebtedness incurred by another person or government.

Budget authority may be classified by its duration (one-year, multiple-year, or no-year), by the timing provided in the legislation (current or permanent), by the manner of determining the amount available (definite or indefinite), or by its availability for new obligations.

## *Forms of Budget Authority*

### Appropriations

The budget authority to incur obligations and to make payments from the Treasury for specified purposes. An appropriations act is the most common means of providing appropriations, but authorizing and other legislation also may make appropriations.

Appropriations do not represent cash actually set aside in the Treasury for the purposes specified in the appropriations act. They represent amounts that agencies may obligate during the period of time specified in the respective appropriations acts. An appropriation may make funds available from the general fund, special funds, or trust funds.

Certain types of appropriations are not counted as budget authority because they do not provide authority to incur obligations. Among these are appropriations to liquidate contract authority (legislation to provide funds to pay obligations incurred against contract authority), to redeem outstanding debt (legislation to provide funds for debt retirement), and to refund receipts.

Sometimes appropriations are contingent upon the occurrence of some other action specified in the appropriation law, such as the enactment of a subsequent authorization or the fulfillment of some action by the executive branch. (*See also* Appropriations Act; Expired Budget Authority *under* Availability for New Obligations *under* Budget Authority.)

### Borrowing Authority

Budget authority enacted to permit an agency to borrow money and then to obligate against amounts borrowed. It may be definite or indefinite in nature. Usually, the funds are borrowed from the Treasury, but in a few cases, agencies borrow directly from the public.

### Contract Authority

Budget authority that permits an agency to incur obligations in advance of appropriations, including collections sufficient to liquidate the obligation or receipts. Contract authority is unfunded, and a subsequent appropriation or offsetting collection is needed to liquidate the obligations.

The Food and Forage Act (41 USC 11) and the Price-Anderson Act (42 USC 2210) are examples of such authority.

### Offsetting Receipts and Collections

A form of budget authority that permits agencies to obligate and expend the proceeds of offsetting receipts and collections. The Congressional Budget Act of 1974, as amended by the Budget Enforcement Act (BEA) of 1990, defines offsetting receipts and collections as negative budget authority and the reductions to it as positive budget authority. In the president's budget, OMB reports offsetting receipts as appropriations.

## Duration

### One-Year Authority

Budget authority available for obligation only during a specific fiscal year that expires at the end of that fiscal year. It is also known as *fiscal-year budget authority* or *annual budget authority*.

### Multiple-Year Authority (Multiyear)

Budget authority available for a fixed period in excess of one fiscal year. This authority is generally available for full fiscal years (e.g., two-year authority), but it may cover periods that do not coincide with the start or end of a fiscal year. For example, the authority may be available from

July 1 of one fiscal year through September 30 of the following fiscal year, a period of 15 months. This type of multiple-year authority is sometimes referred to as *forward funding*.

#### No-Year Authority

Budget authority that remains available for obligation for an indefinite period. A no-year appropriation is usually identified by language such as "to remain available until expended."

#### Reappropriation

Legislation permitting an agency to obligate, whether for the same or different purposes, all or part of the unobligated portion of budget authority that has expired or would otherwise expire if not reappropriated. In the president's budget, reappropriations of expired balances are counted as new budget authority or balance transfers depending on the year for which the amounts are reappropriated.

### *Timing of Legislative Action*

#### Current Authority

Budget authority made available by Congress for the fiscal year or years during which the funds are available for obligation.

#### Permanent Authority

Budget authority that is available as the result of previously enacted legislation and is available without further legislative action. For example, the authority to retain and use offsetting receipts tends to be permanent authority. Such budget authority can be the result of substantive legislation or appropriations acts.

### *Determination of Amount*

#### Definite Authority

Budget authority that is stated as a specified sum at the time the authority is enacted. This type of authority, whether given by an appropriations act or other law, includes directives "not to exceed" a specified amount.

#### Indefinite Authority

Budget authority that at the time of enactment is for an unspecified amount. Indefinite budget authority may be appropriated as all or part of the amount of proceeds from the sale of financial assets, the amount necessary to cover obligations associated with payments, or the receipts from specified sources, the exact amount of which is determinable only at some future date. Or the appropriation may allow the obligation of "such sums as may be necessary" for a given purpose.

### *Availability for New Obligations*

#### Expired Budget Authority

Budget authority that is no longer available to incur new obligations but is available for an additional five fiscal years for disbursement of obligations properly incurred during the budget authority's period of availability.

Unobligated balances of expired budget authority remain available for five years to cover legitimate obligation adjustments or obligations that were properly incurred during the budget authority's period of availability but the agency failed to record. (See 31 USC 1552(a), 1553(a).) (*See also* Expired Account; Unobligated Balance *under* Obligational Authority; Warrant.)

#### Unexpired Budget Authority

Budget authority that is available for incurring new obligations.

## BUDGETARY RESOURCES

An amount that can be used to enter in to new obligations and to liquidate them. Budgetary resources are made up of new budget authority (including direct spending authority provided in existing statute and obligation limitations) and unobligated balances of budget authority provided in previous years. (*See also* Budget Authority.)

## CLOSED (CANCELED) ACCOUNT

An appropriation account whose balance has been canceled. Once balances are canceled, the amounts are not available for obligation or expenditure for any purpose. An account available for a definite period (a fixed appropriation account) is canceled five fiscal years after the period of availability for obligation ends. An account available for an indefinite period (a no-year account) is canceled if the head of the agency concerned or the president determines that the purposes for which the appropriation was made have been carried out, and no disbursement has been made against the appropriation for two consecutive fiscal years. (*See also* Expired Account; Obligational Authority.)

## COLLECTIONS

Funds received by the federal government during the fiscal year. Collections are classified into three major categories: (1) governmental receipts (also called budget receipts or federal receipts), (2) offsetting collections, and (3) offsetting receipts. Governmental receipts result from the exercise of the government's sovereign powers. Offsetting collections and receipts result from businesslike transactions with the public or transactions between appropriated activities. Offsetting collections and offsetting receipts are recorded as offsets to spending. They are called offsetting collections when the collections are authorized by law to be credited to expenditure accounts. Otherwise, they are deposited in receipt accounts and called offsetting receipts.

For further discussion, see "Federal Receipts and Collections" in the Analytical Perspectives section of the president's budget.

### *Governmental Receipts*

Collections from the public based on the government's exercise of its sovereign powers, including individual and corporate income taxes and social insurance taxes, excise taxes, duties, court fines, compulsory licenses, and deposits of earnings by the Federal Reserve System. Gifts and contributions (as distinguished from payments for services or cost-sharing deposits by state and local governments) are also counted as governmental receipts. Total governmental receipts include those specifically designated as off-budget by provisions of law. Total governmental receipts are compared with total outlays in calculating the budget surplus or deficit.

## Offsetting Collections

Collections authorized by law to be credited to appropriation or fund expenditure accounts. They result from businesslike transactions or market-oriented activities with the public, intragovernmental transfers, and collections from the public that are governmental in nature but required by law to be classified as offsetting. Collections resulting from businesslike transactions with the public and other government accounts are also known as *reimbursements*.

Laws authorizing offsetting collections make them available for obligation to meet the account's purpose without further legislative action. However, it is not uncommon for annual appropriations acts to include limitations on the obligations that can be financed by these collections. The authority to obligate and spend offsetting collections is a form of budget authority. The Congressional Budget Act of 1974, as amended by the 1990 Budget Enforcement Act, defines offsetting collections as negative budget authority and the reductions to the offsetting collections as positive budget authority.

Offsetting collections include reimbursements, transfers between federal and trust fund accounts, offsetting governmental collections, and refunds.

### Reimbursement

When authorized by law, an amount collected for materials or services furnished to the public or other government accounts. (For accounting purposes, earned reimbursements are also known as *revenues*.) These offsetting collections are netted against gross outlays in determining net outlays from such appropriations.

### Transfers between Federal and Trust Fund Accounts

Transfers of resources between federal and trust fund accounts are treated as expenditure transfers regardless of the nature of the transaction. The receiving account reports offsetting collections from federal sources (for offsetting collections) or intragovernmental receipts (for offsetting receipts).

#### Offsetting Governmental Collections

A term used by OMB to designate offsetting collections from nonfederal sources that are governmental in nature but are required by law to be credited to expenditure accounts.

#### Refund

A payment made in error and returned to the government. It is credited to the appropriation originally charged. (*See also* Offsetting Collections *under* Collections.)

### *Offsetting Receipts*

Collections that are offset against gross outlays but are not authorized to be credited to expenditure accounts. Offsetting receipts are deposited in receipt accounts. Like offsetting collections, they result from businesslike transactions or market-oriented activities with the public, intragovernmental transfers, and collections from the public that are governmental in nature but required by law to be classified as offsetting receipts.

Offsetting receipts are offsets to gross budget authority and outlays, usually at the agency or subfunction level, but some are undistributed and are offsets to budget authority and outlays in the aggregate. Unlike offsetting collections, offsetting receipts cannot be used without being appropriated. Trust fund offsetting receipts are permanently appropriated and,therefore, can be used without subsequent annual appropriation legislation. (*See* Permanent Authority *under* Timing of Legislative Action *under* Budget Authority; Trust Fund Receipt Account *under* Trust Fund Accounts *under* Account in the President's Budget *under* Account.)

The Congressional Budget Act of 1974, as amended by the Budget Enforcement Act (BEA) of 1990, defines offsetting receipts and collections as negative budget authority and the reductions to the offsetting receipts and collections as positive budget authority. (*See also* Earmarking; Reimbursement.)

#### Proprietary Receipts from the Public

Collections from outside the government deposited in receipt accounts that result from the government's business-type or market-oriented activities. Among these are interest received, proceeds from the sale of property and products, charges for nonregulatory services, and rents and royalties.

Such collections may be credited to general fund, special fund, or trust fund receipt accounts and are offset against budget authority and outlays. In most cases, such offsets are at the agency and subfunction level, but some proprietary receipts are deducted from total budget authority and outlays for the government as a whole. An example of the latter is rents and royalties on the Outer Continental Shelf. (*See also* Earmarking.)

### Intragovernmental Transfers

Collections from other federal government accounts, often as payment for goods or services provided. Most offsetting receipts from intragovernmental transfers are offset against the budget authority and outlays of the agency or subfunction that produced the goods or services. However, two kinds of intragovernmental transfers are classified as undistributed offsetting receipts: payments made to employee retirement trust funds by agencies in their role as employers, and interest received by trust funds.

These offsetting receipts appear as offsets to budget authority and outlays for the government as a whole, rather than at the agency level.

Intragovernmental transfers may be intrabudgetary (on-budget), off-budget, or between on-budget and off-budget accounts. Intrabudgetary transfers are further subdivided into three categories: interfund transfers, in which the payment is made from one fund group, either federal or trust, to a receipt account in the other fund group; federal intrafund transfers, in which the payment and receipt both occur within the federal fund group; and trust intrafund transfers, in which the payment and receipt both occur within the trust fund group.

### Offsetting Governmental Receipts

A term used by OMB to designate receipts that are governmental in nature (e.g., tax receipts, regulatory fees, and compulsory user charges) but are required by law to be classified as offsetting.

## COMMITMENT

An administrative reservation of allotted funds, or of other funds, in anticipation of their obligation. For federal proprietary accounting, a commitment may manifest an intent to expend assets (e.g., to provide government social insurance benefits). See Statement of Federal Financial Accounting Standards (SFFAS) No. 25, "Basis for Conclusions," paragraph 8, and SFFAS No. 17, "Basis for Conclusions," paragraphs 65 and 94. (*See also* Allotment; Obligation.)

## CONTINUING APPROPRIATION/CONTINUING RESOLUTION (CR)

An appropriations act that provides budget authority for federal agencies, specific activities, or both to continue in operation if Congress and the president have not completed action on the regular appropriations acts by the beginning of the fiscal year.

Enacted in the form of a joint resolution, a continuing resolution is passed by both houses of Congress and signed into law by the president. A continuing resolution may be enacted for the full year, up to a specified date, or until regular appropriations are enacted. A continuing resolution usually specifies a maximum rate at which obligations may be incurred, based on levels specified in the resolution. For example, the resolution may state that obligations may not exceed the current rate or must not exceed the lower of the amounts provided in the appropriation bills passed in the House or Senate. If enacted to cover the entire fiscal year, the resolution will usually specify the amount of funds provided for each appropriation account. (*See also* Appropriations Act; Joint Resolution; Supplemental Appropriation.)

## COST

The price or cash value of the resources used to produce a program, project, or activity.

This term is used in many different contexts. When used in connection with federal credit programs, it means the estimated long-term cost to the government of a direct loan or loan guarantee, calculated on a net present value basis over the life of the loan, excluding administrative costs and any incidental effects on governmental receipts or outlays.

In federal proprietary accounting, cost is the monetary value of resources used or sacrificed or the liabilities incurred to achieve an objective.

In economic terms, it is a measure of what must be given up in order to obtain something, whether by purchase, exchange, or production. Economists generally use the concept of opportunity cost, which is the value of all the things that must be forgone or given up to obtain something. The opportunity cost measure may, but will not always, equal the monetary outlays used to measure accounting costs. Economists sometimes distinguish between the private costs of a good or activity to the consumer or producer and the social costs imposed on the community as a whole.

## CREDIT FINANCING ACCOUNT.

A nonbudgetary account (or accounts) associated with each credit program account that holds balances, receives the subsidy cost payment from the credit program account, and includes all other cash flows to and from the government resulting from direct loan obligations or loan guarantee commitments made on or after October 1, 1991. It disburses loans, collects repayments and fees, makes claim payments, holds balances, borrows from the Department of the Treasury, earns or pays interest, and receives the subsidy cost payment from the credit program account.

## CURRENT RATE

As used in a continuing resolution, the *current rate* is the total amount of budget authority that was available for obligation for an activity during the fiscal year immediately preceding the one for which the continuing resolution is enacted. Congress often uses the current rate as part of a formula to indicate the level of spending it desires for a program for the duration of the continuing resolution. The current rate does not allow agencies to fund new initiatives, programs, or both requested for the current year unless Congress specifically authorizes that they be funded. (*See also* Continuing Appropriation/Continuing Resolution (CR).)

## DEBT, FEDERAL

Generally, the amount borrowed by the government from the public or from government accounts. Federal debt may be categorized for reporting purposes as gross federal debt, debt held by government accounts, debt held by the public, and debt subject to statutory debt limit.

For a fuller discussion of federal debt, see *Federal Debt: Answers to Frequently Asked Questions—An Update* (GAO-04-485SP).(*See also* Borrowing Authority *under* Forms of Budget Authority *under* Budget Authority.)

### *Debt Held by Government Accounts (Intragovernmental Debt)*

Federal debt owed by the federal government to itself. Most of this debt is held by trust funds, such as Social Security and Medicare. OMB contrasts it to debt held by the public by noting that it is not a current transaction of the government with the public; it is not financed by private saving and thus does not compete with the private sector for available funds in the credit market; and it does not represent an obligation to make payments to the public.

### *Debt Held by the Public*

That portion of the gross federal debt held outside the federal government. This includes any federal debt held by individuals, corporations, state or local governments, the Federal Reserve System, and foreign governments and central banks. Debt held by government accounts (intragovernmental debt) is excluded from debt held by the public. Debt held by the public is not the same as public debt or Treasury debt.

## DEFERRAL OF BUDGET AUTHORITY

Temporary withholding or delaying of the obligation or expenditure of budget authority or any other type of executive action, which effectively precludes the obligation or expenditure of budget authority. A deferral is one type of impoundment. Under the Impoundment Control Act of 1974 (2 USC 684), budget authority may be deferred only to provide for contingencies, to achieve savings or greater efficiency in the operations of the government, or as otherwise specifically provided by law. Budget authority may not be deferred for policy or any other reasons.

Deferrals may be proposed by agencies but must be communicated to Congress by the president in a special message. Deferred budget authority may be withheld without further action by Congress. Congress may disapprove a deferral by law. A deferral may not extend beyond the end of the fiscal year of the budget authority's availability. However, for multiyear funds, the president may rereport the deferral the next fiscal year. Deferred budget authority that is disapproved by Congress must be made available immediately. Agencies must release all other deferred budget authority with sufficient time remaining in the fiscal year to prudently obligate that budget authority before the end of the fiscal year. (*See also* Apportionment; Impoundment; Rescission.)

## DEFICIENCY APPORTIONMENT

As provided for in the Antideficiency Act (31 USC 1515), an apportionment by OMB indicating the need for supplemental budget authority to permit payment of pay increases to civilian and military employees and military retirees as required by law.

In addition, the head of an executive branch agency may request a deficiency apportionment if a new law is enacted that requires unanticipated expenditures beyond administrative control or an emergency arises involving the safety of human life or the protection of property. Approval of a request for such an apportionment does not authorize agencies to exceed available resources within an account. (*See also* Antideficiency Act; Apportionment; Deficiency Appropriation; Supplemental Appropriation.)

## DEFICIENCY APPROPRIATION

An appropriation made to pay obligations for which sufficient funds are not available. The need often results from violations of the Antideficiency Act. Though technically distinct from a supplemental appropriation, Congress has stopped passing separate deficiency appropriations, so the distinction has become obscured since the 1960s.

## DEOBLIGATION

An agency's cancellation or downward adjustment of previously incurred obligations. Deobligated funds may be reobligated within the period of availability of the appropriation. For example, annual appropriated funds may be reobligated in the fiscal year in which the funds were appropriated, while multiyear or no-year appropriated funds may be reobligated in the same or subsequent fiscal years. (*See* Reobligation.)

## DEPRECIATION

The systematic and rational allocation of the acquisition cost of an asset, less its estimated salvage or residual value, over its estimated useful life. Depreciation reflects the use of the asset during specific operating periods in order to match costs with related revenues when measuring income or determining the costs of carrying out program activities.

## DISBURSEMENT

An amount paid by a federal agency, by cash or cash equivalent, during the fiscal year to liquidate government obligations. *Disbursement* is used interchangeably with the term *outlay*. In budgetary usage, *gross disbursements* represent the amount of checks issued and cash or other payments made, less refunds received. *Net disbursements* represent gross disbursements less income collected and credited to the appropriation or fund account, such as amounts received for goods and services provided. (*See also* Outlay; Expenditure.)

## EARMARKING

Either of the following:

- Dedicating collections by law for a specific purpose or program. Earmarked collections include trust fund receipts, special fund receipts, intragovernmental receipts, and offsetting collections credited to appropriation accounts. These collections may be classified as budget receipts, proprietary receipts, or reimbursements to appropriations.

- Designating any portion of a lump-sum amount for particular purposes by means of legislative language. Sometimes, the term *earmarking* is colloquially used to characterize directives included in congressional committee reports but not in the legislation itself. (*See also* Special Fund Account *under* Federal Fund Account *under* Account in the President's Budget *under* Account; Trust Fund Account *under* Account in the President's Budget *under* Account; Offsetting Collections *under* Collections; Proprietary Receipts from the Public *under* Offsetting Receipts *under* Collections.)

## ECONOMY ACT

A common reference to sections 1535 and 1536 of Title 31 of the *U.S. Code* that provides general authority for one agency or unit thereof to obtain goods and services from another agency or unit. Payment may be made in advance or upon the provision of the goods and services ordered.

## EXPENDITURE

The actual spending of money; an outlay.

## EXPENSE

Outflow or other depletion of assets, incurrence of liabilities, or a combination of both during some period as a result of providing goods, rendering services, or carrying out other activities related to an entity's programs and missions, the benefits from which do not extend beyond the present operating period.

## EXPIRED ACCOUNT

An account within the Treasury to hold expired budget authority. The expired budget authority retains its fiscal year (or multiyear) identity for an additional five fiscal years. After the five-year period has elapsed, all obligated and unobligated balances are canceled, the expired account is closed, and all remaining funds are returned to the general fund of the Treasury and are thereafter no longer available for any purpose.

(*See* Expired Budget Authority *under* Availability for New Obligations *under* Budget Authority.)

## FISCAL YEAR

Any yearly accounting period, regardless of its relationship to a calendar year. The fiscal year for the federal government begins on October 1 of each year and ends on September 30 of the following year; it is designated by the calendar year in which it ends. For example, fiscal year 1990 began October 1, 1989, and ended September 30, 1990. (Prior to fiscal year 1977, the federal fiscal year began on July 1 and ended on June 30. The three-month period July 1, 1976, to September 30, 1976, between fiscal years 1976 and 1977, is called the transition quarter (TQ).)

### *Budget Year*

A term used in the budget formulation process to refer to the fiscal year for which the budget is being considered. With respect to a session of Congress, the budget year is the fiscal year of the government that starts on October 1 of the calendar year in which that session of Congress begins.

### *Current Year*

A term used in the budget formulation process to refer to the fiscal year immediately preceding the budget year under consideration.

### *Outyear*

In the concurrent resolution on the budget, or in the president's budget submission, any fiscal year (or years) beyond the budget year for which projections are made.

### *Prior Year*

The fiscal year immediately preceding the current year.

### *Program Year*

Describes the authorized operating period of a particular program. The term is usually used to distinguish the program's operating period from the federal government's fiscal year. For example, a program year may begin on July 1 of a year and end on June 30 of the following year. Thus, program year 2003 began on July 1, 2003, and ended on June 30, 2004.

## FIXED APPROPRIATION ACCOUNT

An account in which appropriations are available for obligation for a definite period. A fixed appropriation account can receive appropriations available for obligation for one year (an annual account) or for a specified number of years (a multiyear account). (For a distinction, *see* No-Year Authority *under* Duration *under* Budget Authority.)

## GRANT

A federal financial assistance award making payment in cash or in kind for a specified purpose. The federal government is not expected to have substantial involvement with the state or local government or other recipient while the contemplated activity is being performed. The term *grant* is used broadly and may include a grant to nongovernmental recipients as well as one to a state or local government, while the term *grant-in-aid* is commonly used to refer only to a grant to a state or local government. The two major forms of federal grants-in-aid are block and categorical.

Block grants are given primarily to general-purpose governmental units in accordance with a statutory formula. Such grants may be used for a variety of activities within a broad functional area. Examples of federal block grant programs are the *Omnibus Crime Control and Safe Streets Act of 1968*, the *Housing and Community Development Act of 1974*, and the grants to states for social services under title XX of the *Social Security Act*.

Categorical grants may be used only for specific programs or for narrowly defined activities. They may be formula or project grants. Formula grants allocate federal funds to states or their subdivisions in accordance with a distribution formula prescribed by law or administrative regulation. Project grants provide federal funding for fixed or known periods for specific projects or the delivery of specific services or products.

## IMPOUNDMENT

Any action or inaction by an officer or employee of the federal government that precludes obligation or expenditure of budget authority. There are two types of impoundments: deferrals and proposed rescissions. Not all delays in obligating funds are deferrals. Sometimes obligation delays are due to legitimate programmatic reasons or are the result of outside forces not under the agency's control. For example, an agency administering a grant program might receive no grant applications, so no grants can be made. (*See also* Rescission.)

## INTERNAL CONTROL

An integral component of an organization's management that provides reasonable assurance that the following objectives are being achieved: effectiveness and efficiency of operations, reliability of financial reporting, and compliance with applicable laws and regulations. Safeguarding of assets is part of all three of these objectives.

## JOINT RESOLUTION

A form of legislation (designated with S.J.Res. or H.J.Res.) that is either:

- A congressional action typically used to deal with matters such as a single appropriation for a specific purpose, increasing the statutory limit on the public debt, or continuing appropriations. There is no real difference between a bill and a joint resolution; both require a majority vote and become law in the same manner, that is, by bicameral enactment and signature of the president.
- A congressional action used to propose amendments to the U.S. Constitution. Adoption of a joint resolution to propose a constitutional amendment requires a two-thirds majority vote by both the Senate and the House and is not presented to the president for approval. A proposed amendment becomes effective only when ratified by three-fourths of the states.

(*See also* Continuing Appropriation/Continuing Resolution (CR).)

## LIMITATION

A restriction on the amount, purpose, or period of availability of budget authority. Although limitations are most often established through appropriations acts, they may also be established through authorization legislation. Limitations may be placed on the availability of funds for program levels, administrative expenses, direct loan obligations, loan guarantee commitments, or other purposes. (*See also* Administrative Division or Subdivision of Funds; Apportionment; Appropriations Act; Authorizing Legislation; Duration *under* Budget Authority.)

## LINE ITEM

In executive budgeting, a particular expenditure, such as program, subprogram, or object class. For purposes of the concurrent budget resolution, *line item* usually refers to assumptions about particular programs or accounts implicit but not explicit in the budget resolution. In appropriations acts, it usually refers to an individual account or part of an account for which a specific amount is available. (*See also* Obligated Balance *under* Obligational Authority.)

## LIQUIDATING APPROPRIATION

An appropriation to pay obligations incurred pursuant to substantive legislation, usually contract authority. A liquidating appropriation is not recorded as budget authority.

## OBLIGATION

A definite commitment that creates a legal liability of the government for the payment of goods and services ordered or received, or a legal duty on the part of the United States that could mature into a legal liability by virtue of actions on the part of the other party beyond the control of the United States. Payment may be made immediately or in the future.

An agency incurs an obligation when it places an order, signs a contract, awards a grant, purchases a service, or takes other actions that require the government to make payments to the public or from one government account to another. The standards for the proper reporting of obligations are found in section 1501(a) of Title 31 of the *U.S. Code*. See also OMB Circular A-11.

## OBLIGATIONAL ACCOUNTING

The accounting systems, processes, and people involved in collecting financial information necessary to control, monitor, and report on all funds made available to federal entities by legislation, including permanent, indefinite appropriations as well as appropriations enacted in annual and supplemental appropriations laws that may be available for one or multiple fiscal years. It is through obligational accounting that agencies ensure compliance with fiscal laws, including the Antideficiency Act and statutes related to the purpose and period of availability of appropriations.

Obligational accounting rests on the central concepts of the obligation and disbursement of public funds, as those terms are defined in this glossary. The Antideficiency Act, codified in part at sections 1341, 1514, and 1517, and the provisions of section 1501 (commonly referred to as the recording statute) of the *U.S. Code* provide the fundamental components of obligational accounting. Obligational accounting is sometimes also referred to as *fund control accounting*, *appropriation accounting*, and *budgetary accounting*. (*See also* Administrative Division or Subdivision of Funds; Antideficiency Act; Apportionment; Disbursement; Obligation.)

## OBLIGATIONAL AUTHORITY

The sum of:

- Budget authority enacted for a given fiscal year;
- Unobligated balances of amounts that have not expired, brought forward from prior years;
- Amounts of offsetting collections to be credited and made available to specific funds or accounts during that year; and
- Budget authority transferred from other funds or accounts.

The balance of obligational authority is an amount carried over from one year to the next if the budget authority is available for obligation in the next fiscal year. Not all obligational authority that becomes available in a fiscal year is obligated and paid out in that same year. Balances are described as obligated, unobligated, or unexpended.

### *Obligated Balance*

The amount of obligations already incurred for which payment has not yet been made. Technically, the obligated balance is made up of the unliquidated obligations. Budget authority that is available for a fixed period expires at the end of its period of availability, but the obligated balance of the budget authority remains available to liquidate obligations for five additional fiscal years. At the end of the fifth fiscal year, the account is closed, and any remaining balance is canceled.

Budget authority available for an indefinite period may be canceled and its account closed if it is specifically rescinded by law, or if the head of the agency concerned or the president determines that the purposes for which the appropriation was made have been carried out, and disbursements have not been made from the appropriation for two consecutive years. (*See also* Duration *under* Budget Authority; Fixed Appropriation Account.)

### *Unobligated Balance*

The portion of obligational authority that has not yet been obligated. For an appropriation account that is available for a fixed period, the budget authority expires after the period of availability ends, but its unobligated balance remains available for five additional fiscal years for recording and adjusting obligations properly chargeable to the appropriations period of availability.

For example, an expired, unobligated balance remains available until the account is closed to record previously unrecorded obligations or to make upward adjustments in previously under-recorded obligations, such as contract modifications that are properly within scope of the original contract. At the end of the fifth fiscal year, the account is closed and any remaining balance is canceled.

For a no-year account, the unobligated balance is carried forward indefinitely until (1) specifically rescinded by law, or (2) the head of the agency concerned or the president determines that the purposes for which the appropriation was made have been carried out, and disbursements have not been made from the appropriation for two consecutive years. (*See also* Duration *under* Budget Authority; Expired Account; Expired Budget Authority *under* Availability for New Obligations *under* Budget Authority; Fixed Appropriation Account.)

### *Unexpended Balance*

The sum of the obligated and unobligated balances.

## OMB CIRCULAR A-11

Document published by the Office of Management and Budget that provides detailed guidance to executive departments and establishments for preparing and submitting the president's budget and executing the budget.

## OUTLAY

The issuance of checks, disbursement of cash, or electronic transfer of funds to liquidate a federal obligation. Outlays also occur when interest on the Treasury debt held by the public accrues and when the government issues bonds, notes, debentures, monetary credits, or other cash-equivalent instruments in order to liquidate obligations. Also, under credit reform, the credit subsidy cost is recorded as an outlay when a direct or guaranteed loan is disbursed.

An outlay is not recorded for repayment of debt principal, disbursements to the public by federal credit programs for direct loan obligations and loan guarantee commitments made in fiscal year 1992 or later, disbursements from deposit funds, and refunds of receipts that result from overpayments.

Outlays during a fiscal year may be for payment of obligations incurred in prior years (prior-year obligations) or in the same year. Outlays,therefore, flow in part from unexpended balances of prior-year budgetary resources and in part from budgetary resources provided for the year in which the money is spent.

Outlays are stated as both gross and net of offsetting collections. (*See* Offsetting Collections *under* Collections.) Total government outlays include outlays of off-budget federal entities. (*See also* Expenditure; Expense.)

## PROGRAM

Generally, an organized set of activities directed toward a common purpose or goal that an agency undertakes or proposes in order to carry out its responsibilities. Because the term has many uses in practice, it does not have a well-defined, standard meaning in the legislative process. It is used to describe an agency's mission, functions, activities, services, projects, and processes. (*See also* Program, Project, or Activity (PPA).)

## PROGRAM, PROJECT, OR ACTIVITY (PPA)

An element within a budget account. For annually appropriated accounts, OMB and agencies identify PPAs by reference to committee reports and budget justifications; for permanent appropriations, OMB and agencies identify PPAs by the program and financing schedules that the president provides in the detailed budget estimates in the budget submission for the relevant fiscal year. Program activity structures are intended to provide a meaningful representation of the operations financed by a specific budget account—usually by project, activity, or organization.

## REAPPORTIONMENT

A revision of a previous apportionment of budgetary resources for an appropriation or fund account. OMB reapportions just as it apportions. Agencies usually submit requests for reapportionment to OMB as soon as a change becomes necessary due to changes in funds available, program requirements, or cost factors. For exceptions, see OMB Circular A-11, section 120. This approved revision would ordinarily cover the same period, project, or activity covered in the original apportionment. (*See also* Allotment; Apportionment.)

## RECEIPTS

*See* Governmental Receipts *under* Collections.

## REFUND

Either the return of money that the government improperly collected or collected in excess of the amount owed (for example, money owed to taxpayers by the government when their total tax payments are greater than their total tax) or money returned as an appropriation by outside sources for payments that the government made in error, overpayments, or adjustment for previous amounts disbursed. (*See also* Refund *under* Offsetting Collections *under* Collections.)

## REIMBURSEMENT

A sum that is received by an agency as a payment for commodities sold or services furnished to the public or to another government account and that is authorized by law to be credited directly to specific appropriation and fund accounts. Reimbursements between two accounts for goods or services are usually expenditure transactions or transfers.

Anticipated reimbursements are, in the case of transactions with the public, estimated collections of expected advances to be received or expected reimbursements to be earned. In transactions between government accounts, anticipated reimbursements consist of orders that are expected to be received but have not yet been accepted. Agencies cannot obligate against anticipated reimbursements without specific statutory authority. (*See also* Reimbursement *under* Offsetting Collections *under* Collections.)

## REOBLIGATION

Obligation of deobligated funds for a different authorized use. (*See also* Deobligation.)

## REPROGRAMMING

Shifting funds within an appropriation or fund account to use them for purposes other than those contemplated at the time of appropriation; the shifting of funds from one object class to another within an appropriation or from one program activity to another. While a transfer of funds involves shifting funds from one account to another, reprogramming involves shifting funds within an account. (For a distinction, *see* Transfer.)

Generally, agencies may shift funds within an appropriation or fund account as part of their duty to manage their funds. Unlike transfers, agencies may reprogram without additional statutory authority. Nevertheless, reprogramming often involves some form of notification to the congressional appropriations committees, authorizing committees, or both. Sometimes committee oversight of reprogramming actions is prescribed by statute and requires formal notification of one or more committees before a reprogramming action may be implemented.

## RESCISSION

Legislation enacted by Congress that cancels the availability of budget authority previously enacted before the authority would otherwise expire.

The Impoundment Control Act of 1974 (2 USC 683) provides for the president to propose rescissions whenever the president determines that all or part of any budget authority will not be needed to carry out the full objectives or scope of programs for which the authority was provided. Rescissions of budget authority may be proposed for fiscal policy or other reasons.

All funds proposed for rescission must be reported to Congress in a special message. Amounts proposed for rescission may be withheld for up to 45 calendar days of continuous session while Congress considers the proposals. If both houses have not completed action on a rescission bill rescinding all or part of the amount proposed by the president for rescission in the president's special message within 45 calendar days of continuous session, any funds being withheld must be made available for obligation.

Congress may also initiate rescissions. Such congressional action occurs for various reasons, including changing priorities, program terminations, excessive unobligated balances, offsets, and program slippage. (*See also* Apportionment; Impoundment; Rescission Bill *under* Rescission.)

### *Rescission Bill*

A bill or joint resolution to cancel, in whole or in part, budget authority previously enacted by law. Rescissions proposed by the president must be transmitted in a special message to Congress. Under section 1012 of the Impoundment Control Act of 1974 (2 USC 683), unless both houses of Congress complete action on a rescission bill within 45 calendar days of continuous session after receipt of the proposal, the budget authority must be made available for obligation. (*See also* Rescission.)

## REVOLVING FUND

A fund established by Congress to finance a cycle of businesslike operations through amounts received by the fund. A revolving fund charges for the sale of products or services and uses the proceeds to finance its spending, usually on a self-sustaining basis. Instead of recording the collections in receipt accounts, the budget records the collections and the outlays of revolving funds in the same account. A revolving fund is a form of permanent appropriation. (*See also* Public Enterprise Revolving Fund Account *under* Federal Fund Account *under* Account in the President's Budget *under* Account.)

## SUPPLEMENTAL APPROPRIATION

An act appropriating funds in addition to those already enacted in an annual appropriations act. Supplemental appropriations usually provide additional budget authority when the need for funds is too urgent to be postponed until enactment of the regular appropriation bill. Supplementals may sometimes include items not appropriated in a regular bill for lack of timely authorization.

## TAX

A sum that legislation imposes upon persons (broadly defined to include individuals, trusts, estates, partnerships, associations, companies, and corporations), property, or activities to pay for government operations. The power to impose and collect federal taxes is given to Congress in Article I, Section 8, of the U.S. Constitution.

Collections that arise from the sovereign powers of the federal government constitute the bulk of governmental receipts, which are compared with budget outlays in calculating the budget surplus or deficit. (*See also* Governmental Receipts *under* Collections.)

## TRANSFER

The shifting of all or part of the budget authority in one appropriation or fund account to another. Agencies may transfer budget authority only as specifically authorized by law. For accounting purposes, the nature of the transfer determines whether the transaction is treated as an expenditure or a nonexpenditure transfer. (*See also* Allocation. For a distinction, *see* Reprogramming.)

### *Expenditure Transfer*

For accounting and reporting purposes, a transaction between appropriation and fund accounts that represents payments, repayments, or receipts for goods or services furnished or to be furnished.

When the purpose is to purchase goods or services or otherwise benefit the transferring account, an expenditure transfer/transaction is recorded as an obligation/outlay in the transferring account and an offsetting collection in the receiving account.

If the receiving account is a general fund appropriation account or a revolving fund account, the offsetting collection is credited to the appropriation or fund account. If the receiving account is a special fund or trust account, the offsetting collection is usually credited to a receipt account of the fund.

All transfers between federal funds (general, special, and nontrust revolving funds) and trust funds also are treated as expenditure transfers.

### *Nonexpenditure Transfer*

For accounting and reporting purposes, a transaction between appropriation and fund accounts that does not represent payments for goods and services received or to be received but rather serves only to adjust the amounts available in the accounts for making payments. However, transactions between budget accounts and deposit funds will always be treated as expenditure transactions because the deposit funds are outside the budget.

Nonexpenditure transfers also include allocations. These transfers may not be recorded as obligations or outlays of the transferring accounts or as reimbursements or receipts of the receiving accounts. For example, the transfer of budget authority from one account to another to absorb the cost of a federal pay raise is a nonexpenditure transfer. (*See* Allocation; *see also* Transfer Appropriation (Allocation) Accounts *under* Accounts for Purposes Other Than Budget Presentation *under* Accounts.)

## TRANSFER AUTHORITY

Statutory authority provided by Congress to transfer budget authority from one appropriation or fund account to another.

## UNLIQUIDATED OBLIGATIONS

The amount of outstanding obligations or liabilities.

## USER FEE/USER CHARGE

A fee assessed to users for goods or services provided by the federal government. User fees generally apply to federal programs or activities that provide special benefits to identifiable recipients above and beyond what is normally available to the public. User fees are normally related to the cost of the goods or services provided. Once collected, they must be deposited into the general fund of the Treasury, unless the agency has specific authority to deposit the fees into a special fund of the Treasury. An agency may not obligate against fees collected without specific statutory authority. An example of a user fee is a fee for entering a national park.

From an economic point of view, user fees may also be collected through a tax such as an excise tax. Because these collections result from the government's sovereign powers, the proceeds are recorded as governmental receipts, not as offsetting receipts or offsetting collections.

In the narrow budgetary sense, a toll for the use of a highway is considered a user fee because it is related to the specific use of a particular section of highway. Such a fee would be counted as an offsetting receipt or collection and might be available for use by the agency.

Alternatively, a highway excise tax on gasoline is considered a form of user charge in the economic sense, but because the tax must be paid regardless of how the gasoline is used and because the tax is not directly linked with the provision of the specific service, it is considered a tax for purposes of the budget and is recorded in the budget as a governmental receipt. (*See also* Offsetting Collections *under* Collections.)

## WARRANT

An official document that the secretary of the Treasury issues upon enactment of an appropriation that establishes the amount of funds authorized to be withdrawn from the central accounts that the Treasury maintains. Warrants for currently unavailable special and trust fund receipts are issued when requirements for their availability have been met. (For a discussion of availability, *see* Availability for New Obligations *under* Budget Authority.)

## WORKING CAPITAL FUND

A type of intragovernmental revolving fund that operates as a self-supporting entity and conducts a regular cycle of businesslike activities. These funds' functions are financed entirely by the fees charged for the services they provide, consistent with their statutory authority. (*See also* Intragovernmental Revolving Fund Account *under* Intragovernmental Fund Account *under* Federal Fund Account *under* Account in the President's Budget *under* Account.)

---

The Glossary consists of excerpts from GAO-05-734SP, *A Glossary of Terms Used in the Federal Budget Process*, U.S. Government Accountability Office, September 2005.

# Index